Best Wishes
To friends of ?
& Howard C.

A Pleasant Gale on My Lee

Enjoy

A Notable Era in the History
of the Pamlico Area and Outer Banks.

John Morgan 2005

*Heave-ho m'lads,
th' wind blows free,
a pleasant gale is on our lee...
(Old Sea Ditty)*

Copyright © 2001 John Morgan

All Rights Reserved. No part of this book may be used, reproduced or transmitted in any form or by any means, electronic or mechanical, including photocopy, recording or any information storage or retrievals system, without the express written permission of the publisher, except where permitted by law.

ISBN Number 1-880849-31-3
Library of Congress Catalog 2001088609

Manufactured in the United States of America
05 04 03 02 01   10 9 8 7 6 5 4 3 2

To
Geneva
And Our Sons
Johnny
And
Richard

ACKNOWLEDGMENTS

So many people have encouraged me to put together this material and publish it in a book. For all their help I am grateful. In the beginning, Della Robbins had helpful suggestions and ideas she shared on how to arrange the material. Later, Tricia Scott Woolard, at Beaufort County Community College, was of invaluable assistance when she volunteered to lay it out in final form. Without her aid, we would have been lost. We're also indebted to Buddy Swain and Jim Boyd who took us into their arms and invited us to place excerpts on their web site, HatterasOnMyMind.com. And then there's Geneva, my loving wife of 50 years, who kept asking, "When're you going to work on your book some more? You're not getting any younger, you know!" I couldn't have done it without her encouragement and help. While all this was going on, Geneva and I have been active in the Beaufort County Mental Health Association, a volunteer agency organized in the early 1960's as an advocacy mental health program for the citizens of Beaufort County. Our mission is to promote mental health awareness, provide mental health education, and improve the care and treatment of the mentally ill. Our primary focus is educational advocacy on behalf of the mentally ill in the community, while trying to eliminate the stigma that surrounds mental illness. After publishing costs are recouped, any and all proceeds from this work will go into the Beaufort County Mental Health Association's Endowment Fund.

Table of Contents

Acknowledgments   II
Foreword   IX-X
Sea Fever   XI

Part One
Chapter One

Early Development   1
Urban Renewal   9

Chapter Two

Working At An Early Age   11

Chapter Three

Auto Accident   15

Chapter Four

Going To College   19
Matriculation   20
Exposed To Learning   22
First Topcoat   23
War Comes   26
Old East   27

Chapter Five

Dr. & Mrs. Frank Graham   29

Town Hall Meeting	31
Square Dances	32

Chapter Six

Flunked Out	35

Part Two
Chapter One

Happy Times	39
The Ethel Burns	41
Ocracoke Connection	43
Hatteras Development Company	45
State Operated Ferry	46

Chapter Two

Pleasant Cruises	47
Rough Seas	53

Chapter Three

The "Bonnie Belle"	57
Uncle Harvey	61
Uncle Preston	64

Part Three
Chapter One

Ice Houses	67
Law Enforcement	74

Chapter Two

Legendary Tom Angell   77

Chapter Three

Dave Driscoll, Pilot   81
Soup Bowl Haircut   81
The Gaskins Boys   82

Chapter Four

Making A Living   85
Charlie Mason Pogey Boat   91
Interesting Paradox   93
Sport Fishing   93

Chapter Five

Taking in Washing   95
Earn Your Keep   97

Part Four
Chapter One

The Pilot of Hatteras   103
September Storms   106
1944 Hurricane   108
1954 Hurricane Hazel   117

Chapter Two

Shipwrecks	119
The Schooner "Cox"	119
The "Carroll A. Deering"	119
Cannibalism	120
Cape Hatteras Lighthouse	122

Chapter Three

Interesting Documents	127
(Depositions in Old Deed Books	
Beaufort County Courthouse)	

Part Five
Chapter One

Sense of Humor	133
Best Shot	134
Next Best Shot	135
All Wet	135
Dippin' & Chewin'	136
Sources of News	137
Plenty of Gas	138
What's In A Name?	139

Chapter Two

Making Your Own Amusement	141
Banker Ponies	142
Family Song Fests	143
Going To Church	143

Fun In A Sailskiff	145
Homemade Sailboat	147
Summer Baseball Games	148
A Summer Sunday's Outing	149

Part Six
Chapter One

Changes Take Place	151
Began As Challenge	152
Ambassador Speaks	154
Appeared To Be Doomed	156
Consults With Umstead	157
Formal Dedication Cape Hatteras National Seashore	158
Dedication Oregon Inlet Bridge	160

Afterword	167
Index	169

Photos — Illustrations

Page:
3	Fowle's Dock
5	Launching at Pamlico Shipyard
6	Eureka Lumber Company
6	Tug "Eureka"
6	"Dorothy Leigh" Freight Boat
38	Capt. Irv Stowe
40	Irv & Janette Stowe
43	"Bessie Virginia"
45	The "Hadeco" in Hatteras Harbor
46	State Operated Ferry
48	Pamlico Lighthouse
51	Buoy Tender "Linden"
58	The "Bonnie Belle"
60	Utility Skiff
62	Harvey Doxey Stowe
65	The "Miss Yvonne" Under Construction
68	Ice House
69	Rance Oden
70	Hatteras Post Office
72	Main Intersection Hatteras Village circa 1939
73	Dolph Burrus
71	Mary Styron Akers
83	Mending Nets
94	"Albatross I"
102	Janette Stowe
108	Hurricane Flags
113	Richard Dailey
122	Cape Hatteras Lighthouse
150	Fishing Fun
152	Lindsay C. Warren
161	Herbert C. Bonner
166	Wright Memorial

FOREWORD

Growing up during the Great Depression of the 1930's wasn't so bad in this part of the world, especially if you got to spend summers at Hatteras with loving maternal grandparents and other kinfolk. I was born with salt water in my veins and have always had a deep and abiding love for the Outer Banks and its people. When I get to the south side of Oregon Inlet my brogue changes to a drawling Elizabethan accent that distinguishes the Outer Banker from the mainlander. I have always spoken their language, and they mine. Upon my return to Washington following summer vacations at Hatteras, people, after hearing me speak, would immediately say they knew where I had spent the summer!

In the paragraphs that follow I have attempted to present life as seen through the eyes and experiences of a young lad who grew up around the Washington waterfront and was first taken to Hatteras by his Grandmom at 18 months aboard the freight boat that ran from Washington each week. My grandparents were people of simple means but provided well for a family of seven living children of whom my mother was the oldest.

Outer Bankers are proud people with a proud heritage that comes of the sea, by the sea and for the sea where their forebears either protected the coastline through enlistment in the Lifesaving Service, which later became the Coast Guard, or eked out a living by fishing, crabbing and clamming. The past 50 years have seen many changes in the villages comprising the Outer Banks with the coming of paved roads, bridges, and the National

Seashore Park. Commercial fishing has changed to sports fishing, motels and hotels dot the coastline, condominiums have sprung up in all available spaces, and people are employed in entirely different manners than their forebears.

One of my favorite poems is "Sea Fever" by English poet laureate John Maesfield. It captures in the poet's words my feelings as I cross Oregon Inlet and head south that last 50 miles down N C Highway 12 to Hatteras.

SEA FEVER

By John Maesfield

I must go down to the seas again, to the lonely sea and the sky,
    And all I ask is a tall ship and a star to steer her by,
And the wheel's kick and the wind's song and the white sails shaking,
    And a grey mist on the sea's face and a grey dawn breaking.

I must go down to the seas again, for the call of the running tide
    Is a wild call and a clear call that may not be denied;
    And all I ask is a windy day with the white clouds flying,
And the flung spray and the blown spume, and the sea gulls crying.

    I must go down to the seas again, to the vagrant gypsy life,
To the gull's way and the whale's way where the wind's like a whetted knife;
    And all I ask is a merry yarn from a laughing fellow-rover,
    And quiet sleep and a sweet dream when the long trick's over.

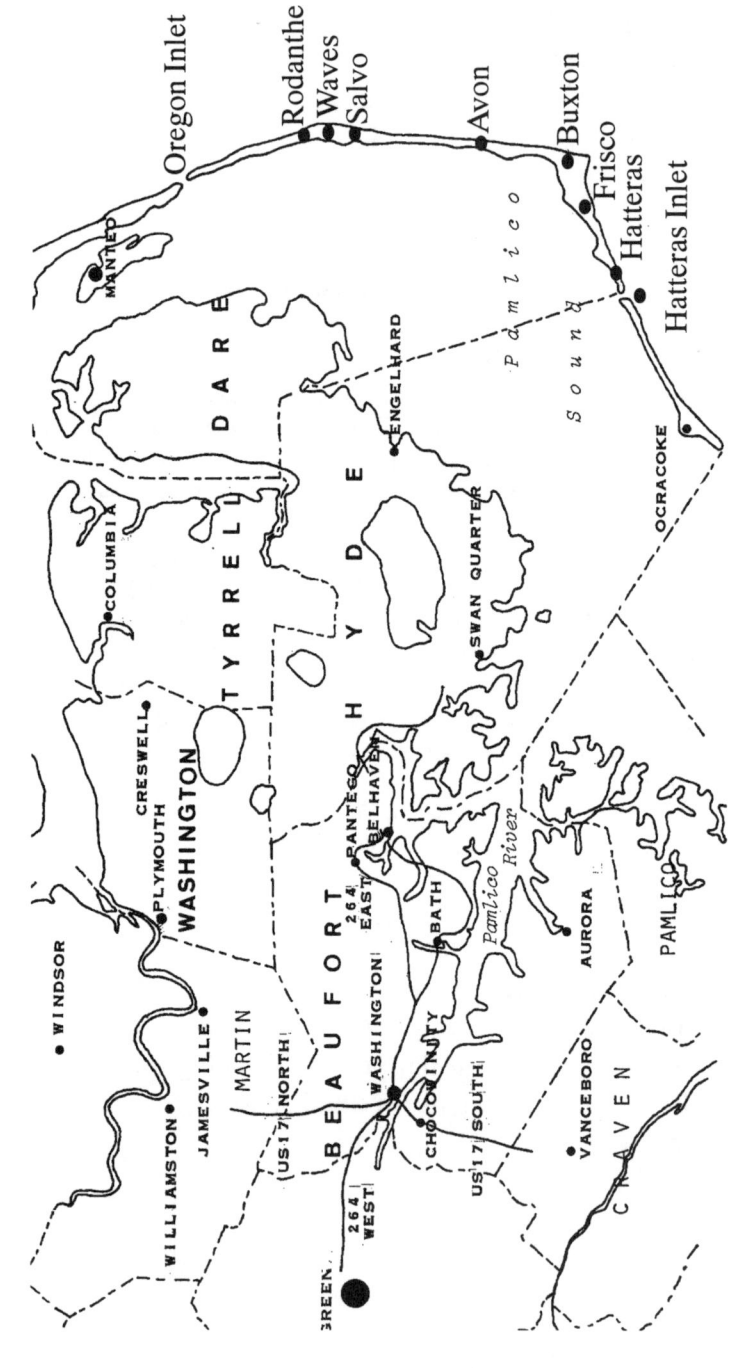

PART ONE

CHAPTER ONE

EARLY DEVELOPMENT

The Pamlico and Tar Rivers played an important part in the early development of Washington, founded in 1776 by Col. James Bonner. It rapidly became a trading center. Bath was the county seat at the time, but because of its deeper water and proximity to upstream villages, Washington continued to grow and in 1785 the General Assembly passed a bill making it the county seat of Beaufort County. In early days sailing vessels plied the waters from Washington to ports of entry at Ocracoke and Hatteras Inlets, south to the West Indies and north to Norfolk, Baltimore, Philadelphia, New York and Boston. Sail finally gave way to steam, and steam to gasoline and diesel engines. Flat-bottomed boats and scows were used in traffic on the Tar River from Washington to Greenville and Tarboro where the water was shallower. Poles were used to propel these craft, and later steam engines would drive side and rear paddle wheelers. In the 1930's the U. S. Corps of Engineers dredged the channel from Blounts Bay to Greenville where a Port Terminal was built to receive cargoes coming through the port of Washington. Spoil areas provide shallow, sandy bars revealed on low tides when the west winds blow.

In the early history of Washington, trade with the West Indies accounted for much of the shipping, while cotton, tobacco, turpentine, tar and lumber made up freight on the flat-bottomed boats going to and from Greenville and Tarboro. Congress made Washington a port in 1790 and a customs house was established. John Gray, Thomas and William Blount were very prominent in early shipping circles. They owned large sailing vessels going to the ports of Europe, West Indies and Northern markets. These ships carried cargoes of cotton, tobacco, lumber and naval stores from here. They returned with molasses, rum, and native goods traded in this area. The Fowle family arrived from New England in the early 1800's, establishing a new mercantile and shipping business. During this time other mercantile houses and ships were owned by John Myers, Joseph Potts and James E. Hoyt. An interesting sidelight about these sailing vessels is that when they did not have a cargo on the return or going out, they required ballast consisting of stones gathered from foreign ports. Many of these stones found their way into the foundations of the homes of this area and in fences surrounding homes and fields. In Bath, the late Rev. A. C. D. Noe would pay the children a cent a piece for all the ballast stones they could find and bring to deposit on a pile kept near the entrance of historic St. Thomas Episcopal Church.

The S. R. Fowle & Co. store, located on West Main street, was known, among other things, for its West Indies molasses. People would bring their own containers to receive the sweet liquid, or, it was put into waxed paper containers furnished by the store in pint and quart sizes. West Indies molasses was lighter and clearer than the "black strap" variety. Many people would use this instead of sugar to sweeten their coffee and tea. The older generation would recall the times when the Fowle schooners would return from the West Indies, causing a large crowd to gather on Fowle's Dock at the foot of Respess Street. Besides molasses these schooners usually had a cargo of bananas, coconuts, and casks of rum. However, the crowd seemed most interested in the molasses. In the unloading of the hogsheads, or barrels, often the bungs

The Fowle warehouse office and dock, located at foot of Respess street in Washington, N. C., before 1900. This is the site of a law firm today. The dock was done away with during the mid 1960's when the bulkhead for Stewart Parkway was being constructed. (Photo Courtesy N. C. Division of Archives and History)

would burst open and the golden liquid would gush forth. Practically all who came brought some kind of container to catch that which was spilled. During this era the Washington waterfront teemed with activity. Businesses were located near the docks since most of the trade was carried on in these areas. The busiest time was during the oyster season when oyster boats would tie up at all available space, often having to double up or triple, going half across the river. When cargoes of oysters were discharged, the skipjacks would then leave for another load of the succulent shellfish to be found in abundance in the many beds beginning in Germantown Bay and Rose Bay in Hyde County, on over on the south side around Bay River and Neuse River, and off Ocracoke and Hatteras. People would stop by one of the many stores located on South Market street in Washington, purchase a bottle of vinegar, salt, pepper, two or three lard trays, and head for the docks to buy a peck or bushel of oysters. There were always people hanging around the docks looking for work, and 15 or 25 cents would hire someone to open oysters in case you didn't want to do it yourself. The Town of Washington used oyster shells to stabilize dirt streets, of which there were many, along with clinkers from the furnaces at the power plant on West Third street, extended. Dust was kept down by spreading used cylinder oil along the dirt streets. This is a "no-no" today.

Large three and four-masters would bring in loads of fish meal to be used in the manufacture of fertilizer. After unloading at the Royster or Phillips Fertilizer factories, they would move over to the Roanoke Railroad and Lumber Co. and Moss Planing Mill docks to take on a load of lumber for the return trip to Norfolk, Baltimore or Philadelphia. During World War II the Phillips Fertilizer property, located at North Shores, became Pamlico Shipyards and manufactured minesweepers. Archie Sanders was president of the company. Following the war the company went into the manufacture of shrimp boats which were ferried to points on the East Coast and Gulf Coast. Grandpop Irv and Uncle Preston Stowe delivered several of these shrimp boats to the Louisiana

Coast, going down the Inland Waterway, through Cedar Keys, Florida, and on out into the Gulf of Mexico. They'd return home on either the train or a bus, pick up another delivery, and head South again.

Launching of the first of a fleet of fishing boats at Pamlico Shipyard, Washington, N. C., following World War II when the shipyard built minesweepers for the war effort. Left to right: Archie Sanders, President of Pamlico Shipyard; Edmund H. Harding, Washington Chamber of Commerce; W. K. Maier, shipyard official; Rena (Peepie) Harding, daughter of Edmund and later married to Julian Davenport, who was the sponsor and broke bottle of champagne over bow; Mrs. Archie Sanders; R. P. MacKenzie, Mayor of Washington, N. C.; Roy J. Wittick of General Seafoods, contractor for the fleet of fishing boats. (Photo Courtesy N. C. Division of Archives and History)

Archie Sanders was president of Pamlico Shipyard and W. K. Maier was a company officer. The occasion of the launching of the first boat of a fleet was a gala event with Edmund H.

The Eureka was a steam-powered tug boat which towed log rafts from points along the Pamlico River to Eureka Lumber Co. in Washington. The tugs were done away with when trucks and trailers were used to haul the logs to the mill. (Photo courtesy Tom Blount collection)

The Eureka Lumber Co. was located at the West End of Washington where the present day Washington Harbor residential district is situated. This view is taken from the log pound. (Photo courtesy Tom Blount collection)

The "Dorothy Leigh" was a familiar sight when docked at the NBC (Norfolk-Baltimore-Carolina) dock located at Water and Bonner streets in Washington. This vessel would bring shipments of sugar from Norfolk, Va. to what was referred to as "the sugar warehouse" during the 1930's and 1940"s. (Photo courtesy Tom Blount collection)

Harding, noted promoter of the Washington Tobacco Market and the local Chamber of Commerce, being on hand to MC the occasion. His daughter, Rena (Peepie) Harding, (later married to Julian Davenport), was the sponsor and broke a bottle of champagne over the bow of the trawler. Also on hand was Washington Mayor R. P. (Mack) MacKenzie, Mrs. Archie Sanders, and Roy J. Wittick of General Seafoods, purchaser of the fleet. The shipyard, after fulfilling its mission, finally went out of business and the only vestige remaining of the docks today are pilings which protrude from the waters off North Shores.

The NBC line (Norfolk, Baltimore and Carolina) operated boats between Norfolk and Washington, bringing large shipments of sugar stored in the "sugar warehouse" at the foot of Bonner street next to Bill Warner's railways. Warner, besides operating the railways, also had a tug boat named "Riverview" which plied up and down the river picking up towing jobs here and there. Eureka Lumber Co. operated two tugs, the "Eureka" driven by steam, and the "Gordon" which was diesel powered. They would pull rafts of logs to the log pound where they were stored and debarked before going to the mill for sawing into lumber, which was then shipped out on barges. In the case of the earlier sailboats bringing in fertilizer and leaving with lumber, large river barges later took the place of the sailing vessels. They were pushed, or towed, by tugs. These were done away with when log trucks brought in timber which was cut from large tracts owned by Eureka Lumber Co., John L. Roper Lumber Co. and Bates Lumber Co. Eureka eventually sold all its holdings to N. C. Pulp Co. in the early 1950's, and N. C. Pulp was absorbed by Weyerhaeuser Co. a short time later.

An oyster factory was located at the foot of Bonner street and oyster shells were ground into a powder to be used in the manufacture of fertilizer. In recent years disease has decimated the oyster harvests in this area and in Chesapeake Bay, and they're getting more difficult to come by each year.

In early days ground oyster shells were used in making cement. When the old Beaufort County Courthouse was restored in 1973-74, the white paint was removed from the red brick and to make the mortar for re-pointing the brick more authentic, ground oyster shells were mixed in with the cement. Many old bricks disintegrated when sandblasted, but fortunately there were enough extra bricks under the courthouse to replace those lost.

The excavation for the new Beaufort County Courthouse in 1970 revealed shell fossils indicating a time when an inland sea covered the area. Aurora has a fossil museum where a wealth of material dredged from the Texasgulf (now PCS Phosphate) mines is on display.

Following occupancy of the new Beaufort County Courthouse in September 1972, several groups interested in historic preservation came together and petitioned the Beaufort County Commissioners to save the old courthouse. They were fearful it would meet the same fate as other historic structures and become a parking lot or filling station site. Fund raisers were held in civic clubs, book clubs and local schools, and generous appropriations by the county commissioners made it possible to preserve the historic 1785 structure and continue it in public use. It had been entered in the National Register of Historic Sites, and several proposals were made for its continued use, with the Beaufort-Hyde-Martin Library finally getting approval to occupy the downstairs portion, while the upstairs courtroom was preserved in much the same decor as when it was in full use and is the site today of special meetings, and has been used on occasion to hold sessions of court.

The Bell and Stewart families maintained the clock for generations. In 1954 the works were changed to electrical and the weekly manual winding of the weights that controlled the running and striking mechanisms became automatic. Over the years the electrical motor burned out, some works became worn, and the old clock stopped. There was much interest in getting it working again. Generations of Washington's citizens heard the faithful tolling of the hours by this old clock long before they could even begin to speak. The striking of the old clock reassured everyone and gave them the feeling that "all's well!" A tower clock specialist from Georgia was hired to come up and repair the works, and it worked greatly for about three weeks, then went on the blink again! Efforts to get the Georgia man back failed. Local tower clock buffs want to attempt to get it running again. If this fails, another option would be to remove the old works, showcase them in the lobby of the BHM Library, and install new state-of-the-arts works.

Urban Renewal

As shipping by rail and trucks became cheaper and faster, the Washington waterfront began to fade. The docks began to deteriorate and rot away while businesses moved away from the downtown area and out into places where parking and more modern buildings were available. A government program, Urban Renewal, came into being in the 1960's and through this agency the downtown waterfront was cleared, a 75-foot bulkhead was extended from the existing shoreline, hydraulic fill from the sandy river bottom was dredged in, and a parkway today graces the once rundown riverfront. Thomas Stewart was Mayor of Washington at this time and took a progressive view toward preserving the waterfront and downtown, and clearing other sections of Washington suffering from urban blight. Citizens of Washington can point today to better housing and living conditions for everyone. The thoroughfare appropriately bears the name "Stewart Parkway." Tom says the designation also included his late father, R. Lee Stewart, Sr., who served as mayor, and his grandfather, Ed Stewart, who was mayor earlier in the century.

CHAPTER TWO

WORKING AT AN EARLY AGE

I came along during the era when the Washington waterfront was teeming with activity and prior to when its demise began.

At the age of nine I started selling "The Washington Daily News" in downtown Washington for three cents a copy. I kept one cent and turned in two cents to Leon Roebuck who was in high school and was in charge of street sales. The late Bill Waters was circulation manager. He would let me ride with him to Plymouth or Williamston to deliver papers whenever a delay caused us to miss the bus. The ride to Plymouth was rough in those days because NC 32 had not been paved at that time.

I would hurry from John Small School to the WDN, pick up my armful of papers, and make a dash for Adams Supply Co., a couple of blocks West of Market on Main street, where my Uncle George Morgan clerked. He would give me five cents for a paper most of the time and on occasion, when feeling generous, would cough up a dime! I did this for a couple of years. I'd delivered Uncle George his paper one day when he asked me if I'd be interested in a job in the store paying me $1.50 a week? I was earning from 75 to 90 cents a week selling papers, so naturally I jumped at the chance to almost double my earnings.

At the age of 11 I started work at Adams Supply Co. each afternoon after school and Saturdays. The store stayed open from 7:00 A. M. to 7:00 P. M. weekdays and until 11:00 P. M. Saturdays.

After cleaning up, re-stocking shelves and dressing the windows it would be 12:30 to 1:00 A. M. before I got home on Sunday. Bill Peele was the manager and he was like a father to me. My first job was to sort out rotten Irish potatoes from the good in six barrels located in the basement. It was a stinkin', terrible job, but an appropriate initiation to the grocery business.

I delivered groceries, swept the floor, dusted and stocked the shelves, and did "gopher" jobs for about two years before I was allowed to wait on customers. We'd take orders, the customer would leave to attend to other business or go to the movies, and call for their orders later in the day. Tobacco chewin' and snuff dippin' was in vogue. I remember a hole in the floor next to the flour bin on the left side of the store where people would stand while giving their orders and pause occasionally to spit through that hole. They all had good aim and hardly ever missed! We did a big telephone business where housewives would call in their orders and delivery was made on the bikes.

The lot behind the store was where farmers coming to town on Saturday would park their mules and carts (some had horses) and those who were better off would park their pickups and autos. This was during prohibition and many times I observed people out in the back lot drinking "white lightnin'" from a fruit jar. Some had manufactured it themselves, while others had purchased a pint or quart from one of the many bootleggers who plied their trade in the back lots and alleyways. In 1937 the State of N. C. abolished prohibition and legal ABC stores came into being. Many public meetings were held pitting the anti-liquor groups (especially the Womens Christian Temperance Union) against the pro-ABC forces and you can be assured there were some heated arguments.

James Moore and Grover Freeman, two black men from Wootentown, were the deliverymen throughout the city and Washington Park. Grover's brother, Vernon, worked part-time. Melvin Oden lived on River Road and like me, was a high school student and worked part-time. I always admired Melvin because he went to the Catholic school on Ninth street, graduated with honors, went to college, graduated, and became a successful CPA in New York. I was especially impressed that he went all the way through Virgil and Cicero, while I was having a hard time getting through Virgil under Madame E. T. Campbell, that erstwhile teacher of Latin and French at WHS.

Between deliveries we'd hoss around in the back room. One day Grover had an ice pick aiming it at a spot on the wall and seeing how close he could come to the mark. Next, I got the ice pick and aimed it at Grover's big foot, seeing how close I could come to his shoe. I missed the mark! The ice pick stuck into Grover's big toe. He just stood there glaring at me with incredible disbelief, then broke into a big smile, pulled the pick from his shoe, removed the shoe, bathed the wound in rubbing alcohol, wrapped it, and went on his way. I never again tried to see how close I could come to anybody's feet with an ice pick!

James Moore had a favorite saying that someone had passed on to him. It went like this:

> "My boss man done ordered him a bran' new plane,
> And has offered me a free trip to Spain,
> But I ain't g'wine, I'm g'wine stay right here
>   where I ought to be!

"Suppose that plane was to git over the middle of the ocean
        an' happened to stop!
'Twixt the heaven and the earth and the deep blue sea
        I'd have no place to hop!
And there's liable be a giant whale down there waitin'
        for me,
But I ain't g'wine let that whale make no san'wich
        outta me, 'cause I ain't g'wine --I'm gonna stay
        right here where I ought to be!

"Now the whale swallered Jonah and threw him up
        on the sand,
But if that whale was to get hold of me, I'm liable
        be the WRONG man!
Naw suh, I ain't g'wine -- I'm gonna stay right here
        where I ought to be!"

    James, Grover, Vernon and Melvin were some of the best friends I ever had. We had a good time delivering groceries for Adams Supply Co.

CHAPTER THREE

AUTO ACCIDENT

I missed spending summer vacation at Hatteras in 1938 due to being is an automobile accident on the way back home from a week at Boy Scout Camp Charles near Bailey, N. C. It was June 12, a sunny Sunday afternoon, and we had just deposited Warren "Bigtime" Whichard at his grandmother's home in Grimesland. Lee Whealton was driving. Jimmy Nunnelee had accompanied Lee on the trip up to Bailey. Melvin Whealton, Lee's brother, was in the back seat with me. We headed out of Grimesland in the 1937 Plymouth turret top sedan coming toward Washington when we pulled up behind two autos going at a slower rate of speed.

Seeing the way ahead was clear Lee accelerated to pass when suddenly the car just ahead of us pulled out to pass the lead car, forcing us to the shoulder of the road. All I know from that point is what I was later told. Our car went out of control, careened down the right shoulder, jumped a ditch and turned over four times in a field. I regained consciousness the next day in Room 51 on the third floor of Tayloe Hospital in Washington. The first thing I noticed through the haze of coming to was my right leg suspended from a frame around the bed with a steel pin through the knee and 10-pound weights attached to ropes from the pin and extending over the end of the bed.

The following week I complained of my neck being stiff and aching. X-rays revealed a dislocation of the first and second cervical vertebras. Sandbags were placed on either side of my head and I was told to keep still and not move.

I celebrated my 15th birthday in Room 51. Liz Shelton, daughter of Mr. and Mrs. Warren Shelton who operated a florist shop on West Second street, and some of the kids from our First Baptist Church Sunday School class, came up with a cake and presents. They sang "Happy Birthday" and things were going well until the floor supervisor ran them off because the noise was disturbing other patients on the floor.

After six weeks in traction, a cast was placed on the leg and I went home for the long recuperation. Walking casts were not in use at that time so I was bed-ridden for the next six weeks until the cast came off. During convalescence I had plenty of time on my hands. I read many novels, pulp magazines, westerns, World War I stories, and made flying model airplanes which I would fly down the hall from my bed and crack them up, make repairs, and fly them again.

In November, 1939, while at recess on the school ground, I was tussling with one of my friends when he picked me up and dropped me on my back. The impact shook my entire spinal column and threw me into a quadriplegic trauma. After a few minutes the feeling began to return to my body. It felt like a million pins and needles pricking my skin. I immediately went up to Tayloe Hospital which was only a couple of blocks from the school and saw Dr. R. H. Hackler, the x-ray doctor who checked me out and made arrangements for me to go to Duke Hospital in Durham.

Mrs. Clarence Little was taking her daughter, Sadie, up to Duke for treatments at the time and offered to take my mother and me. We arrived at Duke and I was entered in Welch Ward for a two-week stay in traction. The interns and residents held class around my bed about two or three times a week. I remember the Duke-Carolina football game being played at Duke Stadium the first Saturday I was there, and I was listening over earphones attached to a plug next to my bed. I could hear the roar of the crowd without the earphones. Duke won 6-3. After the two-week stay at Duke my neck was placed in a leather collar and I wore this for six weeks after my return home.

Monnie Adams, Jr., from Chocowinity, was tussling with some fellows at the service station located on the corner of Highways 17 and what was then 264 and snapped a vertebra in his neck. Dr. Josh Tayloe had him in traction at Tayloe Hospital. Dr. Josh called me and asked that I go up to the hospital so he could get a look at my collar. He found a paper sack, tore it open, traced the outline of my collar and directed me to take it to the City Shoe Hospital and ask Herman Eason to make him one like it. He placed this on Monnie's neck before releasing him from the hospital!

Thirty-four years later, December 26, 1973, I returned to Duke for an operation on the neck, spending six weeks this time! Through the years the first and second vertebrae had slipped, causing pressure on the base of my brain which made me lose coordination and control of some of the bodily functions. My doctor advised me to go to Duke since they had treated me before and had a record of when I was a patient. I called it "going into drydock for repairs!" Bone from my hip was fused around the first and second vertebras. A decision was then made to place my head in a halo to mobilize the neck and hold it in position while the bone graft was taking. The halo was anchored at four points around my skull, two in front and two in back. A body cast supported it and I was in it for three months. After removing the halo, I wore a four-poster brace for another six weeks, then a surgical collar for another three weeks before being released by my Duke doctors. Thanks to modern medical skills, at the age of 50 I had gained a new lease on life!

CHAPTER FOUR

GOING TO COLLEGE

When I graduated from Washington High School in May, 1941, I was poor, but proud, and decided I wanted to go to Chapel Hill to further my education. Several lads from Beaufort County had worked their way through with self-help jobs during the Great Depression. I decided if they could, so could I.

I wasn't immune to work, having contributed to my upkeep since the age of nine by selling "The Washington Daily News" on the streets of Washington for three cents a copy and working my way through high school at Adams Supply Co. I decided I could get a job on the campus at UNC and help pay my way along with some help from the State Rehabilitation Commission because of a physical disability resulting from a broken neck in an auto accident at the age of 15.

Joe Tunstall, the pharmacist at Tayloe Drug Store where I was jerking sodas during the summer of 1941, had graduated from the UNC School of Pharmacy a couple of years before, and had held self-help jobs on campus. He advised me to get in touch with Mr. Ed Lanier, Director of Self-Help. I took a day off in the middle of July and hitch-hiked to Chapel Hill to meet Mr. Lanier. He was an affable, pleasant, easy-going gentleman who had come up from Georgia, worked his way through the university, and remained to become director of self-help. After his retirement from University service he served as Insurance Commissioner of North Carolina. When Mr. Ed found out I was a soda jerk he immediately phoned Ray Ritchie, manager of the Book Exchange, and said he'd collared a young soda jerk from down in the Original Washington, N. C., and asked if he could use another jerk when the fall quarter began? Ritchie invited me over for an interview and hired me on the spot. He said I'd start at 30 cents an hour and to report one week before Freshman Orientation and he'd orient me to the Book Ex soda fountain. And he did!

Matriculation

Jim McMullan had lived in Chapel Hill when his father, Hon. Harry McMullan, was Attorney General of North Carolina. Jim graduated in 11 years after spending his final year at a military school. His family had moved back to Washington following his graduation. My father had worked as a clerk in Mr. McMullan's law office and later Mr. Mac got my father a job in the Register of Deeds office working with Mr. Gilbert Rumley. Jim's mother, Miss Patty, told my mother that she'd be happy to give me a lift to Chapel Hill when she took Jim up for matriculation. He had to be there a week early, too. Miss Patty drove one of those nice Lincoln sedans. I thought, "Just think what the guys will say when they see me riding up to the Hill in that big Lincoln!"

I'd never owned a suitcase -- always used a paper box to pack whatever few belongings I needed when spending summer vacation at Hatteras. I found a pasteboard box about the size of a suitcase that would fit in the boot of Miss Patty's Lincoln, got a piece of clothes line and wrapped it around the box to secure it, and we were on our way. I had enough clothes for a couple of changes a week, two sheets, a bedspread, and some toilet articles. Off we went to Chapel Hill to ma-trick-u-late at the University of North Carolina! Jim had nice, fancy luggage which occupied most of the boot. We got along fine and had a nice ride up to Chapel Hill. Miss Patty let me out in front of the Book Ex with my pasteboard box suitcase, and I reported for work right away.

Two veteran workers at the Book Ex took me under their wings to show me the ropes and assisted me in finding a room. Charlie Briley was a tall, light blond with a broad smile and a winning way. He was from Greenville and was majoring in accounting. Frank Alspaugh, from Winston-Salem, was a dapper, handsome young fellow who was a clothes hound and won a prize for being BDMC (Best Dressed Man on Campus). He also was an accounting major.

Briley knew Mrs. Thrall, widow of Dr. Frank Thrall who formerly taught in the English Department, living at 201 Gimghoul Road, and who took in a couple of self-help boys each year to keep her furnace stoked, rake the yard and sweep her porch. Briley called Mrs. Thrall who said she was looking for a couple of boys since her former tenants had left.

After work Briley and Alspaugh accompanied me to the Thrall residence. She had already interviewed another young fellow from Lexington, N. C., named Lewis Foster. She took me down to her basement, showed me the room which was a boarded-off corner next to the furnace with a shower stall located in the opposite corner of the basement, and told me to make myself at home. Lewis and I took a liking to each other right off, being from similar situations and backgrounds. We worked out a schedule of taking turns doing the chores expected of us and checked with Mrs. Thrall two or three times a week for any new instructions. Lewis was a great guy. At the end of our freshman year he was drafted in the Army. Later I got word that he was killed in action.

Exposed to Learning

It's a good thing the entrance requirements at UNC were not as strict in 1941 as today, or there's a good likelihood I would not have been admitted. I credit my high school principal, E. F. Ruble, for my getting out of high school. He exercised great patience with me, since I was somewhat of a discipline problem and many times the teachers would excuse me from the classrooms and order me to go to Mr. Ruble's office. (I've often thought they'd like to tell me to go somewhere else!) I would appear at Mr. Ruble's office door. Knowing what I was there for, he would give me a knowing nod, direct me to sit in a chair in the outer office, crack a textbook and read. "At least you'll be exposed to some learning," he'd say.

Another thing I could thank my stars for was that I was proficient at typing, making straight A's, while making B's on shorthand and bookkeeping. This helped pull up my average on some of the other subjects. I had enough units to qualify for the Commercial Diploma. At this time Washington High School had three levels of curricula -- Classical Scientific for those taking the college preparatory high school course which included higher math, chemistry and physics; Commercial for those taking typing, bookkeeping and shorthand the last two years; and General for those who did not qualify for the first two. Had Mr. Ruble not given me a little nudge in the right direction now and then, there's no telling where I might have wound up! He knew my mother from having taught her at Washington Collegiate Institute (WCI). Maybe he took pity on me because of having known her.

In later years when I was in Mr. Ruble's Sunday School

class at First United Methodist Church in Washington I was still learning from this great teacher and gentleman. From listening to and observing him, I tried to emulate his approach to Sunday School lessons and later became a teacher of the Adult Class which today bears his name. I just hope a little of Mr. Ruble rubbed off on me!

First Topcoat

I held several jobs on the campus at UNC, chief of which was jerking sodas at the Book Ex, considered in 1941-46 as one of the prime self-help jobs. I also ran messages for Miss Mable Mallette from Dean R. B. House's office in South Building. She was the veteran secretary for the dean's office and a very precise person who was in charge of getting inter-office memos from the administrative offices to other offices and the various fraternity and sorority houses. She and Mr. Ed Lanier would get me baby-sitting jobs, too. I also worked during mealtimes at the N. C. Cafeteria on Franklin Street where D. R. Brooks was manager. I got my meals for this work. In the Spring I would sell class rings and graduation invitations, representing the L. G. Balfour Co. I received commissions on my sales.

Ray Ritchie, manager of the Book Ex, was a tough taskmaster and what we would term today as a "workaholic". His assistant was a young fellow from Greenville named Norman Savage. They ran a tight ship. We had to punch in on a time clock located in a corridor just behind the soda fountain. Thirty cents an hour wasn't bad in 1941!

South Building was located just across the court from the Book Ex. There was no toilet facility in the Book Ex building and when we had to go we would run over to use the toilet in the basement of South Building. During cold weather I would run over in my shirtsleeves. Dr. Cecil Johnson, Dean of Students and my freshman advisor, had his office in South and would see me running bare-armed across the Y Court and one day while getting his morning cup of coffee asked me if I had a top coat.

I'd never owned a top coat, so I told the Dean that I never had any use for such a garment -- that I made out very well with a sweater. The next day Dr. Johnson came in for his morning break and told me to go down to Bierman's Department Store and pick up a package they had for me. Lo and behold, it was a new top coat! Dr. Johnson thought I ought to have more protection from the elements up there in Chapel Hill, so he took it upon himself to be my benefactor. That is how I came by the first top coat I ever owned!

And speaking of workaholics, I worked with a fellow from Kinston named Pete Pully. We had a partnership on dance concessions. On the occasion of dance nights we'd pull a shift at the Book Ex, go to Kenan Stadium and get drink troughs, set up on the terrace behind the Patterson Indoor Pool, and have a hat-coat check concession inside Woollen Gym. Since we worked at the Book Ex we had access to a quota from the Durham Coca Cola Bottling Co., and also to cigarettes and candies from the Navy Pre-Flight and V-12 programs -- all rationed items hard to come by in civilian life during World War II. We also held concessions in the Tin Can, a gym located adjacent to Woollen. We worked dances for the University Club, Order of the Grail (of which I was later a member and held the office of Exchequer), Fall and June Germans and various fraternity and sorority dances. This was during the big band era when Tommy Dorsey, Glen

Miller, Harry James, Russ Morgan, Guy Lombardo, Kay Kyser, Hal Kemp, Johnny Long and others would play for campus affairs.

There were a couple of good campus bands, too, made up of fellows who played in the Carolina Marching and Concert bands. Hurst Hatch, a drummer from Raleigh, led one of the musical outfits, while Johnny Satterfield was leader of another. I played baritone horn in the UNC Marching and Concert Bands, but never played with a dance band.

Pete and I would employ young high school students to help us. I remember two of them as being Sam Summerlin who later was an internationally known Associated Press reporter and bureau manager at various locations around the world, and Freddie Bowman, whose father was a lobbyist for the wine and beer industry.

Pete's mother operated a barbecue stand in Kinston and would send him a check for $100 about two or three times a year. He'd tear them into a thousand pieces, exclaiming, "I don't need help from mama!" I tried to get him to endorse them over to me, but he'd have no part of that! Pete had something in him that kept saying, "Drive, drive, drive!" He'd work until he'd fall out from exhaustion (an eye problem had kept him out of the service) and we'd take him to his room, dump him into bed, and leave. He'd get three or four hours rest, and get up ready to go again. That's the kind of guy he was. We had a good working relationship with W. D. Carmichael who was comptroller of the university. Mr. Carmichael got Pete to help him with plans for construction of "The Scuttlebutt" at the corner of Cameron and Columbia streets across from Carolina Inn. It was a soda fountain and notions shop for Pre-Flight and Navy V-12 personnel on campus during World War II. It was razed in 1996; thus, another familiar landmark was gone to make way for newer buildings. Pete got a degree in chemistry, then took another degree in marketing. He later became national sales manager for S. E. Massengill & Co., a pharmaceutical firm. He is now retired and living in his native Kinston, N. C.

WAR COMES

Sunday afternoon, December 7, 1941.

I had been to a movie at the Carolina Theater and while crossing the campus on my way to Gimghoul Road, I heard radios in dormitories crackling out the news. I stopped at the soda fountain in Lenoir Dining Hall where a radio located on the counter was giving rapid-fire details of the bombing by the Japanese of Pearl Harbor. Students were talking about the repercussions and the possibility of the United States going to war with Japan.

On Monday the radio in the Book Ex where I was working carried President Franklin D. Roosevelt's message to a joint session of Congress calling for a declaration of war on this "day that will go down in infamy". It was a somber occasion. A crowd had gathered in the Book Ex and in the lobby of the "Y" to hear Roosevelt. Young men began to make plans to enlist in the Armed Services. A great change came over the campus at The University of North Carolina following December 7, 1941.

Because of the broken neck I had sustained when 15 years old, my local draft board placed me in Four-F. I had been over to Raleigh to try to enlist in the Navy V-12 program which allowed students to remain on campus while getting their military training, but to no avail. I stayed on campus and "fought the battle of Chapel Hill" during World War II. In the summer of 1942 when everyone was leaving for the service, a group of self-help students calling themselves "The Carolina Co-Op" rented a house on Mallette Street, and I roomed with a fellow from Hendersonville, N. C., Ed Shytle, with whom I worked at the Book Ex. He was a member of the varsity basketball team, known then as the "White Phantoms" and coached by Bill Lange who doubled as a Physical Education instructor when not coaching basketball. Coach Bill had us in softball and would always ask me to bring him some Beech Nut chewing tobacco, which assured me of an "A" in his Phys Ed class! Ed was about five-nine and quick on his feet. He had a decent set shot and lettered for the Phantoms. Cam Rodman of Washington played on the same team. Ed graduated at the end of the summer term and joined the Marines. One year later I received a report from his sister, Katherine, who worked in Chapel Hill with Hospital Savings (now Blue Cross-Blue Shield), that Ed was killed in action on Saipan.

OLD EAST

In the fall of 1942 I moved into Old East dorm just across from the "Y" Court and closer to my work at the Book Ex. Francis Nordan from Smithfield roomed across the way in Old West. We would get up at 5:00 A. M. and go over to make coffee and milkshakes, and prepare to open before the 8:00 o'clock rush. Dick Wallach, a young lad from New Haven, Connecticut, was one of the four guys in the large third-floor room we shared. I was awakened by Dick each morning to make sure I got over to the job on time. Two guys from Asheville, Ed Clark and Jim Mason, were the other roommates. Dick later moved to the ZBT Fraternity. Ed and Jim entered the Navy V-12 program and later shipped out. Nordan went into the Air Force and became a bomber pilot in the European Theater of Action.

Richard Adler, author and composer, was a reporter on "The Daily Tar Heel". He heard that I was from the Outer Banks and did a feature article for the DTH concerning some of my experiences at Hatteras. I often think of this as I read and hear of the smash successes on Broadway authored by Adler. He has been a great benefactor of the University and retired in Chapel Hill.

CHAPTER FIVE

Dr. and Mrs. Frank Graham

I spent six weeks during the summer of 1943 rooming at a private home on Franklin Street located next to the president's mansion. I learned that University President Dr. Frank Graham and his wife had two rooms at the rear of the mansion and would take in four self-help students to help around the house with chores such as keeping the furnace stoked, the yard raked and the porch swept. I applied to Mrs. Graham for a spot in one of the rooms and was accepted along with Cy Whitfield, a young fellow from Hurdle Mills, N. C. in Person County, who was in pre-med and studied at the library most of the time. I was working such odd hours that we didn't get to see much of each other. Hubert Robinson was caretaker of the premises and served as chauffeur for Dr. Graham. He supervised us and pointed out each day our responsibilities. In later years Hubert was a familiar figure as the receptionist in the lobby of Morehead Planetarium. He served on the Chapel Hill Town Council and was highly-respected in the community.

Dr. Frank was on the War Labor Board and would spend weekdays in Washington, D. C. He would board a Seaboard Coastline Pullman on Friday evenings, arriving early on Saturday in Raleigh where I would meet him with the University auto whenever Hubert Robinson was not available. He was short of stature and never drove. Miss Marian would always have a hot breakfast of bacon and eggs, toast and coffee on the table for us, and she'd have a cup of tea "for a little stimulation". We'd always catch up on the latest happenings at these breakfast gatherings. One of my jobs was to drive him whenever he was home. During these times together we got to know each other on a personal basis. Dr. Frank had a brilliant mind. It was always said that he was about 20 years ahead of his time. I was struck by his humility and his uncanny ability to remember names. His Sunday night "fireside chats" at the mansion drew many students to share with this great mind. He could see them years later and call them by name.

A staunch Presbyterian, Dr. Frank would attend the University Presbyterian Church and many times I would accompany him. It was just a short walk from the mansion. The Rev. Charles Jones was pastor. The congregation included many professors and had a liberal leaning. It was said that Rev. Jones was also about 20 years ahead of his time, but he filled the pews each Sunday morning. Miss Marian, on the other hand, was a devout Episcopalian. Her father, Dr. Drane, was rector of the historic Edenton Episcopal Church at that time. She would attend the Episcopal Church of the Cross which was located just a few paces west of the mansion next to Spencer Womens Dorm. The Grahams were like mother and father to me during the two and one-half years I lived at the mansion. I shall never forget them.

Dr. Frank was appointed in 1949 by Governor Kerr Scott to fill the unexpired term of J. Melville Broughton, former North Carolina governor who was a U. S. Senator and died in office. Graham was defeated in his bid for a regular term in a bitter second primary by Willis Smith of Raleigh in 1950. On April 30, 1951, Graham was appointed by the United Nations Security Council as UN representative for India and Pakistan where he rendered outstanding service for 19 years before resigning in 1970 due to declining health.

The Grahams loved to spend summer vacations at Nags Head. I remember driving up from Hatteras one summer afternoon in 1960 and seeing Dr. Frank walking beside the highway with his head buried in a newspaper. I drove up beside him, stopped and greeted him. He slowly looked up from his paper and said, "Well, if it isn't John Morgan"!

Miss Marian died April 27, 1967 in New York. Her funeral was held from the Church of the Cross in Chapel Hill with burial in the Chapel Hill cemetery. Dr. Frank moved back to Chapel Hill after his retirement and lived with his sister, Mrs. Kate Sanders. He died February 16, 1972. His funeral was held from the University Presbyterian church and he was buried beside his beloved Marian.

Town Hall Meeting Of The Air

George V. Denny, Jr., was moderator of "The Town Hall Meeting of the Air" over a national radio network in the late 1930s and 1940s. Denny was a University graduate and had ties with Eastern North Carolina and was a good friend of Dr. Frank Graham. He arranged to hold a "Town Hall Meeting" broadcast on the campus of Womens College at Greensboro in 1944, and Dr. Frank was invited to attend.

I drove Dr. Frank over to Greensboro. On the way he said, "Now, John, people might be reluctant to ask questions to get the program started, so when we get there I want you to stand and ask the first question and that will get others in the mood to ask more".

"What should I ask?" I inquired.

It had to do with the war effort and what was being done on the home front to help. I wrote it down on a small piece of paper, and when Mr. Denny saw my hand fly up he recognized me, asked my name and where I was from and then called for the question. I learned later that Dr. Frank had briefed Mr. Denny over the phone that I would be asking the first question. And that was the first and only time I ever appeared on national radio. I later worked with local stations WRRF and WHED in Washington, but was never on a national network program.

Square Dances at the "Y"

During my freshman year at UNC Dean R. B. House would play his harmonica at square dances on the "Y" Court, with Bill Cochrane and Fish Worley, a couple of mountain boys, calling the sets. Bill and Fish graduated in 1942. I had learned enough by listening to them and participating in square dancing to be able to call sets. Each week during the Fall we would use recorded western and hillbilly music, along with Dean House's mouth harp, and have a big square dance session. Occasionally there would be live music, but mostly recorded. We'd count off in odd and even couples, with odds moving on and evens standing still -- eight hands around and circle right, half and back to the left -- right hand across and circle left, left hand across and circle right -- swing your opposite and then your own. Birdie in the cage and circle left -- birdie out and possum in and circle right. Now promenade! And so it went with variations -- weave the basket, east meet west and kiss her hard -- north meet south and do the same -- wind the clock -- promenade -- form another big circle and go through routine again. Clogging sprang out of this earlier style of square dancing and is popular throughout the state today. You sort of made your own entertainment in those days. The juke box in the "Y" played all the big band favorites of the day.

CHAPTER SIX

FLUNKED OUT

At one time I was working in the Book Ex, the N. C. Cafeteria, dance concessions from two to three times a month, working for my room, selling class rings and invitations, and any other odd jobs I could pick up along the way. I flunked out of the School of Commerce and Dean Dudley DeWitt Carroll called me to his office. "Morgan," he said, "I've been checking up on you. It appears you're working full time and going to school on the side. It's supposed to be the other way around. I suggest you go home, get a job, save your money, and come back to apply for re-admission. I'm sure we'll look favorably upon your request".

I left the University early in 1945 and came home. Fate connected me with WRRF radio station where I got my first experience in that media. Working with Uncle Rufus Armstrong and his brother, Carl, a couple of old vaudeville actors, and their string band, introduced me to acting and show business, and an appreciation of country and western music and gospel singing. They appeared weekly on Edmund H. Harding's "Washington on the Air" show which promoted the Washington Tobacco Market.

I returned to Chapel Hill in the Fall of 1946. By then the war was over. VE and VJ Days were behind us. GI's were returning to finish their education which had been interrupted by the war, and a new post-war spirit was beginning to pervade the campus. The next blow to my pursuit of higher education then came in the form of reclassification by my local draft board to One-A. I had a friend named George McKee who had one leg shorter than the other that had kept him out of the service. He had been reclassified, too. We went over to Raleigh and enlisted in the regular Navy for a two-year hitch. I didn't bother to officially withdraw from the university and in 1960 I was on campus attending to another matter when I discovered this fact and finally officially withdrew. George and I were sent to Great Lakes Naval Training Station where he was accepted and sent on to boot camp, but I was detained at the receiving center where x-rays were taken of my neck which I had injured in 1938 and which had kept me out of the service up until that time. They kept George but shipped me back, saying I was too big a medical risk. I worked at the receiving center for 30 days while my separation papers were being processed and became friends with Mrs. Ann Miller who was a hostess at the nearby canteen. She lived in Lake Forest, Ill., near the base and befriended me by lending me books to read and playing gin rummy. She was one peach of a lady.

After I got back home the local draft board sent me to Ft. Bragg one more time and another rejection because of the neck injury. I then returned to my job with WRRF. In 1947 a group of local businessmen decided to open another station, offering Uncle Rufus Armstrong the job as manager. Armstrong enticed me to come with him by offering me $5.00 more a week than I was getting, and I signed WHED on the air on July 1, '1948, remaining with the station until June, 1951 when I accepted a job as Sports Editor of "The Washington Daily News" where I remained for 13 and one-half years before being elected Register of Deeds of Beaufort County, taking office on December 7, 1964 and retiring after 28 years on December 7, 1992.

In the Fall of 1948 I was introduced to a young student nurse at Tayloe Hospital School of Nursing. Her name was Geneva Braddy from Bath, and on October 22, 1950, she became my bride. She has been my sweetheart, my lover, my wife, my friend and confidante, the mother of our two sons, and a guiding light in my life. I have often said that whatever I am or ever hope to be, I can attribute to a loving wife who has put up with my shortcomings (of which I have many) while I have not had to contend with her shortcomings (of which she has none)! Whatever it was (other than a blind date) that brought Geneva and me together, be it fate, destiny or mystical powers, I am thankful to the Good Lord that it is my lot to be married to a wonderful person like Geneva.

When Dr. David T. Tayloe returned home to practice pediatrics in 1956, he hired Geneva as his office nurse and she stayed with him for thirty-nine and one-half years. They were an excellent doctor-nurse team and took care of three generations of Beaufort and surrounding counties' babies and youngsters. It can truly be said of both of them that they are "institutions" of the area.

Capt. Irv Stowe

(Photo by Francis Mason of Gettysburg, Pa., circa 1947)

PART TWO

CHAPTER ONE

HAPPY TIMES

I was what some people called a "free spirit" during my upbringing, being streetwise and alleywise and generally getting along well with everyone. All of us had our "happy times" during childhood. My "happy times" consisted of hanging around the waterfront, swimming at the Vandemere and Norfolk-Southern trestles, camping out on the bluffs overlooking Blounts Bay on the south side of Pamlico River, and summer vacations at Hatteras with my maternal grandparents, John Irvin and Janette Stowe. I was named for my maternal grandfather who was known all his adult life as "Cap'n Irv" Stowe. In the late 20's and 30's he was captain of the "Ethel", a supply boat that ran from Hatteras to Elizabeth City once a week, with the cargo consisting of boxes of iced-down fish on the trip up and store goods, lumber and hardware on the return. She also carried passengers.

Travel to and from the Outer Banks was for the most part by water because of being isolated from the mainland by Oregon Inlet to the North, Hatteras Inlet to the South, Pamlico Sound on the West, and the Atlantic Ocean on the East.

Other freight boats during this time included the "Kathleen" which took turns with the "Ethel" on weekly voyages up the Pasquotank River to Elizabeth City and return. Billy Stowe, a cousin of Cap'n Irv, was skipper of the "Kathleen" while Mr. Horton Austin was mate and later captain when Mr. Billy retired. The "Mary Fletcher" ran from Hatteras to Washington each week

Irv and Janette Stowe

and she was captained by Randolph Stowe, another cousin of Cap'n Irv, with Sammy Neal as mate. Alternating with the "Mary Fletcher" on trips to Washington was the "Flossie Muir" captained by Johnny O'Neal with Herbert Oden as mate. The first three mentioned boats were powered with large paraffin (diesel) burning engines, while the Flossie was a two-masted sailboat with a large auxiliary gasoline engine and a yawl boat which hung from stern davits. Later the "Ethel" burned and was replaced by the "Mallison." The " J.E. Sterling" was another freight boat serving the area, along with the H.C. Drewer.

Uncle Edward Scarborough , a native of Avon, married my Aunt Agnes. Edward operated a small freight boat named the "Ruth" and later secured a larger boat named the "Iowa". When the new highway was completed in 1950 Edward purchased a truck for hauling merchandise and fish, and traded between Avon and Elizabeth City and Norfolk.

THE ETHEL BURNS

The "Ethel" burned to the water line before daylight on a July morning in 1936. She was owned by a group Hatteras & Elizabeth City businessmen. Mr. Kit Austin, a neighbor of my grandparents, had been to the scene of the fire and wondered why Irv was not there. Getting concerned, Kit came down to Irv's home and called. Getting no answer he positioned himself beneath the second-floor bedroom window and tried hollering to wake Irv, but to no avail. Finally, he grabbed a handful of gravel from the driveway and threw it against the glass window, and that brought Irv out of his sleep. Upon looking out the window to see who, or what, was causing all the disturbance at this early hour, Irv asked Kit what in the world was going on? "Haven't ye heard?" replied Kit, "the 'Ethel' has burnt slam to the waterline and all that's left of her is the bottom boards. They cut her loose from the dock and she drifted over to the p'int where she went aground"! Grandpop dressed and rushed up to the scene, but it was all over by this time.

It was speculated that young scalawags had stolen some chickens, cleaned them, lit the galley stove, cooked the chickens, and washed down by East Lake corn whisky, had themselves a big party -- but failed to extinguish the fire before leaving. Everyone guessed that the stove over-heated and caught the galley on fire after the party broke up. Passersby discovered the fire and summoned help to cut the "Ethel" loose from the dock to keep it from catching fire. This ended Irv's career as a freight boat captain. He devoted the remainder of his working years to fishing and shrimping with Uncle Harvey, and helped his older son, Preston, with the construction of the "Miss Yvonne". She was built in the hangar of the Gooseville Gun Club, where pilot Dave Driscoll kept his aircraft when on Hatteras. The "Ethel" was later replaced by the "Mallison" which was of similar construction but had a different type of engine-- a two-cylinder monster that went "ka-chook, ka-chook, ka-chook". You could hear her coming from a long distance away.

THE OCRACOKE CONNECTION

Ocracoke had contact with Washington fish houses and merchants. The "Preston", captained by Dave Williams and his brother Phil, was a two-master of much the same build as the "Flossie Muir". Another was the "Relief" operated by Capt. Isaac "Little Ike" O'Neal and his brother, Walter. The "Dryden" was a motor-driven freight boat operated by Capt. Ike O'Neal. Jesse

Garrish was a mate on the "Dryden" as was Sid Tolson. The "Bessie Virginia" was the last freight boat serving the Ocracoke-Washington run until the early 1960's. She was captained by Vann Henry O'Neal with mate Powers (Red) Garrish. Vann Henry later served as Port Captain for the Ocracoke Ferry service.

The "Bessie Virginia"

The last freight boat to run between Ocracoke and Washington was the "Bessie Virginia" shown here at Fowle's Dock at the foot of Respess St. in Washington, circa 1954. left to right: George Currin of Maola Ice Cream Co.; "Red" Garrish, mate; Lee B. "Togo" Wynne, Washington merchant and entrepreneur; Blount O'Neal of O'Neal Electric Co.; Bill Duncan of Maola Ice Cream Co., and Capt. Vann henry O'Neal. (Photo by John Morgan)

Ryon Day operated a freight boat between Washington and ports of call including Durham's Creek, South Creek, Hoboken and points in between. He operated a fish market and crab factory located on Water Street in Washington. His boat caught fire and burned at the mouth of Durham's Creek when going into dry dock for repairs sometime in the early 1950's. Day never replaced this vessel and resigned himself to operating trucks to haul fish and crabs.

43

The Hatteras and Ocracoke freight boats would dock at various locations along the Washington waterfront including S. P. Willis & Sons, located adjacent to the City Market at the foot of Market Street; Sterling's Fish Market located adjacent to the Maola Ice Cream and Coca Cola Bottling plant; the dock at the foot of Market Street just behind the City Market; docks located to the rear of the Crystal Ice Co.; Fowle's Dock, located at the foot of Respess Street, and occasionally at the Pamlico Chemical dock, commonly called "The Pea Dock", at the foot of Gladden Street. They would take on cargoes of block ice used in icing down boxes of fish coming from Hatteras and Ocracoke, drums of oil which took up space on the decks of the boats, food supplies, lumber and hardware items, and other orders which came from merchants and builders along the Outer Banks.

If one had an automobile and wanted to drive to Hatteras, the route usually followed was up Highway 17 to Elizabeth City, on over to Sligo and down through Currituck County to Point Harbor and over to Kitty Hawk where a plank road would take you to Whalebone Junction. This would take the better part of a full day of driving. At this point you could take a right and go over to Manteo and spend the night, or keep heading south to Oregon Inlet where Toby Tillett operated a four-car ferry. A narrow sand road could be traversed after debarking Tillett's craft. If you happened to be going down on low tide, you could take to the low-water mark on the ocean side and make much better time. Otherwise, one had to negotiate the sandy road where more than likely one got stuck three or four times before arriving at one's destination, and it was "get out and push!" Prior to starting on the trip down the beach one would always slacken the tires by letting out air. All autos of this era carried a hand pump and a patch kit for repairing flats.

HATTERAS DEVELOPMENT CO.

The "Hadeco" in Hatteras Harbor circa 1947. (Photo Courtesy N. C. Dep't Archives)

Frazier Peele of Hatteras and Tom Eaton of New Bern established the Hatteras Development Co. around 1936-37 and secured a freight boat which they appropriately named the "HADECO", using the first two syllables from each word in the company logo. This boat made regular runs to Engelhard, taking and bringing fish, supplies, passengers and autos. Milton Meekins was captain and Mr. Isaiah Ballance mate. Peele pioneered ferry service across Hatteras Inlet to Ocracoke Island, this being the forerunner of the state-operated ferry service of today. Peele and Eaton were instrumental in developing the Hatteras Harbor and through the Rural Electrification Administration, brought the first electric power to the village with construction of a power plant which consisted of a diesel-powered turbine to generate the current. Poles were placed and lines strung around the village as the people signed on for this much-awaited service. "Just think," said my grandmother, "no more shades to clean, no more wicks to trim, no more having to fill lamps with kerosene every day"! The plant was later moved to Buxton where it was operated by the Electric Membership Cooperative and power was purchased from Virginia Electric Power Co. which erected transmission lines down the beach from substations to the north.

STATE-OPERATED FERRY

In this 1952 photo we're on one of the first state-run ferries across Hatteras Inlet following the pioneering of Frazier Peele who established the first run across the inlet using a converted barge and later a surplus military landing craft.

CHAPTER TWO

PLEASANT CRUISES

Our trips to Hatteras usually originated from the S. P. Willis dock. We traveled on the "Mary Fletcher" most of the time, although some trips were on the "Flossie Muir". My mother would take my brother, Richard, and me down to the dock and entrust us to Capt. Randolph Stowe and mate Sammy Neal when we traveled on the "Mary Fletcher". Sammy was engineer and his first job was to light the torches to heat the cylinder heads. At the correct temperature the engine would jerk and belch black smoke from its stack, shaking the entire vessel from stem to stern. Then she'd settle down and Cap'n Randolph would back her out into the stream and get under way. After we cleared the Norfolk-Southern trestle and got abreast Grandpap's Island, Sammy would grab my brother and me by our hands and arms, hang us over the stern, and wash our feet. "You're not a-goin' to dirty up my clean sheets," he'd say, referring to the neatly made-up bunks in the main cabin.

As a youngster inquiring about Grandpap's Island, I was told that it came about as a result of spoil from dredging operations when the channel was deepened in that area. At one time the S. P. Willis family entered a claim and had a deed to the island, which later was inherited by Phil Willis, who deeded it to his son Mike. Today the island has eroded to where it is under water, and the few remaining cypress trees support a large flock of cormorants which roost there every evening just before sunset.

Cap'n Randolph taught us about navigation and would let us take a turn at the helm, telling us when to turn a little to the left or right (or as he put it, sta'board and port) while keeping a steady course by the compass nestled in its box in the middle of the control shelf just forward of the large wooden steering wheel with the oak spokes and handles. "Steady as she goes" was heard many times during those pleasant cruises down the Pamlico River, past Pamlico Lighthouse (which was manned in those days) and across Pamlico Sound. Pamlico Light was located just off Pamlico Point on the South Side of the mouth of the river. We remember the lighthouse keeper sitting in his easy chair on the porch, which surrounded the edifice, smoking his pipe and waving as the boat would pass.

Pamlico Point Shoal Light. Screwpile lighthouse placed at mouth of Pamlico River in 1828. View here is from tender with lighthouse at left and skipjack at right. During Civil War federal troops set fire to the structure, but the Confederates put out the fire. (Photo Courtesy Coast Guard Historian)

There were several "screw pile" lighthouses located at strategic points in the sounds and river mouths in Coastal North Carolina. Following his return from Coast Guard service in the Pacific Theater during World War II, my Uncle Berry Stowe was stationed for a short time at the Roanoke Marshes Lighthouse located in Roanoke Sound near Manteo, N. C. This was one of the first screw-pile lighthouses built in the state (around 1856) and was in constant use until it was decommissioned in 1955. A "screw pile" has been described as a piling where the end going into the sand has a broad-bladed screw which is twisted into the sand, with the blade giving more stability to the pile. The lighthouse usually sat atop six or eight of these pilings. Some were six-sided, some eight and some square. I recollect the one at Pamlico Point being six-sided. Davits on one side were used to hoist and lower the small utility boat used in going ashore for supplies. Married lighthouse keepers usually kept their families aboard, so the wife was chief cook and bottle washer, and if there were children, man and wife had to be teachers as well.

All lighthouses along the Outer Banks at this time were using the new Fra-nel lens. According to The Encyclopedia Americana, in 1815 Augustin Fresnel (pronounced Fra-'nell), a young French government engineer, entered upon a career of scientific activity which proved to be of almost unprecedented brilliancy and success as the phenomena of diffraction first engaged his attention and led to what became known as the Fresnel lens in lighthouses along the many coasts throughout the world. He designed a lens which made possible the whole range of dioptric or refractory illumination. His design used the available light more efficiently and concentrated it into a single beam of light. This lens can be described as a curtain of prisms in front of the light source and centered around a bull's-eye lens. The light rays are refracted, or bent, and focused into a horizontal beam far more efficiently than the old reflector systems that had been in use. By adding reflector prisms above and below the source of light, the normally wasted light rays were added to the total illumination. After first being placed in operation at Cordouan, France, his lenses were later manufactured in six different sizes, known as Orders. A First Order lens is like the one installed in the Cape Hatteras Lighthouse at Buxton, N. C. in 1870, being the largest and measuring 12 feet in height and six feet in diameter. Nearly all lighthouses in the United States were equipped with Fresnel lenses. The one atop the Ocracoke Lighthouse is a Fourth Order, and there is another on the Bodie Island Lighthouse just north of Oregon Inlet.

Oil lamps first illuminated these reflecting devices. Later, motor-driven generators supplied electricity both for the houses and the lamps. These were called "Delco plants". Today solar panels supply power for aids to navigation.

Oliver's Reef, located in Pamlico Sound about three miles off Hatteras, was guarded by one of these manned lighthouses which later was stripped of its superstructure and became one of the many skeleton lighthouses in the area. We enjoyed sheepshead fishing around the pilings, using mud fiddlers for bait. As progress mandated battery powered lights at the various locations around the sounds and river mouths, the manned lighthouses were converted to skeleton structures. Coast Guard buoy tenders service aids to navigation today. The "Linden" and later the "Verbena" were stationed at the Washington Buoy Yard which was located adjacent to the Highway 17 bridge. The "Verbena" was moved to Hobucken in a consolidation move during the

1950's. When I was growing up Mr. Tom Grace Willis from Carteret County was keeper of the Washington Buoy Yard. Later came Clyde Farrow from Hatteras and Edison Midgette from Manteo who were among the last keepers of the Washington facility before it was de-commissioned.

The buoy tender "Linden" stationed at the Washington Buoy Yard circa 1937. Note bridge keeper's house on Hwy 17 bridge in background.

Some interesting facts about screw-pile lighthouses have been passed on to me by my life-long friend and high school classmate, the late, Josh Kingsley Wood. His grandfather, George Henry Wood of Perquimmans County, was assistant keeper of the Roanoke Marshes lighthouse in 1881-82. He died in 1922.

A listing of North Carolina's lighthouses located in the inlets, sounds, rivers and channels is as follows:

1826 - Pamlico Point Lighthouse
1856 - Wades' Point
1856 - Croatan
1860 - Northwest Point of Royal Shoal
1860 - Roanoke Marshes
1866 - Federal Point (near New Inlet)
1866 - Oak Island on mouth of Cape Fear River
1867 - Long Shoal
1867 - Harbor Island
1867 - Southwest Point of Royal Shoal
1867 - Mouth of Roanoke River
1868 - Mouth of North River
1868 - Horseshoe Shoal
1869 - Mouth of Neuse River
1874 - Olivers Reef near Hatteras Inlet
1877 - Brant Island Shoal
1880 - Laurel Point in Albemarle Sound
1891 - Gull Shoal on West side of Pamlico Sound

The 13 colonies had their own aids to navigation.

August 7, 1789, Congress passed an act assuming responsibility of all aids to navigation.

The first secretary of the treasury, Alexander Hamilton, administered lighthouses personally.

1792 - Commissioner of Revenue.

1802-1813 - Secretary of Treasury.

1813-1820 - The fifth auditor of the United States, Stephen Pleasonton, was called "general superintendent of lights".

1852-1910 - The lighthouse board was established. There was an inspector in each district (local collectors of customs). This was called The United States Lighthouse Service.

1910-1939 - United States Bureau of Lighthouses -- George R. Putnam.

1939 -- United States Coast Guard.

According to Wood, the screw-pile lighthouses of the inland waters, in the period just before and after the Civil War, were of a conventional square style of construction, making possible the addition of a large upper room, or attic.

Wood has delved into screw-pile lighthouses all along the Maryland and North Carolina inland waters. He says the Chesapeake Bay lighthouses are mostly hexagonal in design, with some octagonal. He has put together authentic scale models of some of these lighthouses, and they are on display and for sale at the Beaufort County Arts Council.

ROUGH SEAS

There were times when a journey across Pamlico Sound was rough. The wind would freshen from the nor'east and whip the waves into a frenzy of white caps. The "Mary Fletcher" had a high bow. She'd rise on the crest of a wave and come down with a mighty thud, parting the waves, with the wash crashing up against the cabin. We would feel a shudder go through her as she began to negotiate another wave. We often wondered if she'd make it.

My brother would get seasick and vomit. Sammy Neal always had a ten-quart water bucket ready for just such a happening. Amazingly I never was susceptible to seasickness and took delight in poking fun at my brother, who said it wasn't funny at all! The water barrel, which usually was full of "wigglers" (mosquito larvae) was located just forward of the mast and the "forepeak" which housed the galley. The donkey engine for raising and lowering cargo in the hold was just forward of the water barrel.
The mate would wrap a heavy line around the revolving wheel on the donkey engine and when he'd tighten up, the line would take hold and lift loads off the dock to be lowered into the hold and vice-versa.

In the late 1930's on a voyage from Washington to Hatteras aboard the "Flossie Muir", mate Herbert Oden decided he'd catch a nap in the jib which was furled around the jib boom, the "Flossie" being under auxiliary power at the time and waiting for the wind to freshen before putting up the sails. We had just passed Pamlico Point Lighthouse and heading pretty well into the sound when Herbert turned over in his sleep and rolled out of the jib, falling under the bow. Capt. Johnny O'Neal was at the helm and saw Herbert fall. With quick presence of mind he jumped into the cabin and turned the power off the engine, knowing that Herbert would be sucked underneath and possibly chewed up by the revolving propeller.

Herbert was "keel-hauled", going from bow to stern, his right leg brushing against the now-stopped propeller and cutting a deep gash in the calf. Mr. Johnny lowered the yawl and picked up his bleeding and weak mate, got him back aboard, soaked a rag with kerosene and bathed the wound, wrapping it in rags and stopping the flow of blood for the time being. There was infection and Dr. Kenfield came within a hair of having to amputate. The leg eventually healed, but Herbert always favored that limb with a slight limp.

CHAPTER THREE

THE BONNIE BELLE

Between trips to Elizabeth City, Grandpop Irv built his sturdy fishing boat, the "Bonnie Belle". He had an earlier boat by the same name -- a surplus Coast Guard lifeboat (sharp both fore and aft), in which he had rigged a six-cylinder Studebaker engine. This craft served him well while fishing the Pamlico Sound and offshore in the Atlantic in the late 20's and early 30's. Grandpop told me about the time a "fruiter" ran aground in Hatteras Inlet in 1929 and Hatterasmen and Ocracockers participated in the salvage operation. Grandpop loaded the surf boat with bananas and came to Washington to sell them. He got $1.00 per stalk or one penny per banana as he sold them from his boat which was berthed at Fowle's Dock at the foot of Respess Street. At this time my family rented an apartment upstairs over Johnson's Printing House, located across Respess Street near First National Bank. He brought us a stalk of the bananas and they were green as a gourd. I remember not being able to wait until they ripened and I got a terrific belly ache from eating those green bananas. Grandpop told the story about the Hatterasman that came to Washington on his first trip away from the Outer Banks and bought his first banana. When asked how he liked it the Hatterasman replied, "Well, h'it was alright but I shore did hate to have to throw away that big core!"

Grandpop was a master carpenter and boatbuilder. He never had to rely on blueprints or templates in the construction of "Bonnie Belle" No. 2. He just drew a profile of the shape he wanted, laid the keel, and proceeded from there. "Bonnie Belle" No. 2 was what was termed in those days as a "huntin' cabin"

The "Bonnie Belle" 40-ft. fishing boat built by Capt. Irv Stowe circa 1935 shown on her maiden voyage to Hatteras Inlet following her launching.

style of construction. He had helped Calvin Burrus build a similar model. She was 40 feet in length. Grandpop had access to top quality juniper and cypress lumber from one of the mills at Elizabeth City, and on each trip up to the Pasquotank Port city he'd pick out choice pieces. Cedar trees grew near the house, and from some of these he fashioned the "knees" for the framing, while the cypress completed the side and bottom timbers. Affixed to this sturdy framework were the juniper planks. All boats at Hatteras during this time were built of these materials since they have a lasting quality and repel worms and other marine infestations. Copper nails were used to fasten all this together, along with brass screws. All insets were filled with beeswax putty. We young'uns were kept busy sharpening planes, hatchets and other cutting tools on the grindstone. One would turn the crank and keep water poured on the stone while the other would hold the instrument to be honed. All shavings and scrap pieces of wood would be kept in a separate pile to be used on wash days to keep the fire under the pot in which the clothes were boiled.

With a majestic flared bow and a curved stern, she was a beauty to behold as she took shape over the months of the summer and fall of 1933 and on into 1934 when at last the big day came for the launching. She was constructed in the back yard of the home place. Water myrtles and live oaks had to be negotiated between the construction site and the landing at soundside, a distance of about 200 feet. Grandpop rounded up family members and other able-bodied men to help. She was gently lowered on jacks from the scaffolding surrounding her to rollers, and the laborious journey from back yard to shoreside began. All the men got along side and behind her and pushed, while others steadied her with poles holding up each side. Good planning had prepared the way, and in short order she was in the water.

The bottom and side boards of select lumber were planed to perfection so that caulking (corkin') was not required. The salt water caused the boards to swell together in a perfect fit so that in two or three days a leak could not be detected. She was tied to a stake about 300 feet from the shoreside. A 12-foot skiff tied closer to shore in knee-deep water was used to get out to the larger boat. Then came the task of installing a newer model Studebaker engine, finishing off the cabin and superstructure, and finally the "shakedown" cruise, the maiden voyage, down to Hatteras Inlet Coast Guard station and back -- and she performed flawlessly. Whoever doubted it would be otherwise? She was rigged for fishing in the sound and ocean. During World War II

Irv worked in the shipyard at Manteo where sub chasers were being built, and his boat served as his home during that time.

Grandpop and Uncle Harvey built a 16-foot skiff from some of the lumber left over from the construction of the "Bonnie Belle". It was used to get from shoreside out to his fishing boat and also to shove up to the main part of the village to go shopping for groceries and supplies, placing them in the skiff and shoving back home. If we'd get into water too deep to shove we'd put

Sixteen foot utility skiff used to get from shore out to where the "Bonnie Belle" was moored to her stake.

the rowlocks in and row. There was quite an art to shoving. One person would get on the port side and one on the starboard, place the oar in the sandy bottom, stand upon the thwart, and come down to the bottom of the skiff with one leg while holding the other on the thwart, repeating this motion and working in tandem to keep the skiff headed in the right direction. If the wind was blowing fresh it would sometimes necessitate both getting on the same side to shove.

Later Uncle Harvey secured a used Briggs-Stratton air-cooled engine of three horsepower, couplings, shaft and propellor, and rigged them in the skiff. We spent many pleasant hours fishing between the village and Hatteras Inlet. Whenever it was flood tide the current was so strong in the channel that the skiff would hardly make headway. Many times we'd stop in a shallow bight about halfway to the inlet and catch gray trout, pinfish and croakers.

UNCLE HARVEY

Uncle Harvey Doxey Stowe was an invalid all his life, living to the ripe old age of 72. He had a deformed body -- a kyphro- scoliosis (hump back), with arms deformed to the elbows and curved legs over which he had little control. He crawled from one place to another. He had a good head on his shoulders and was of invaluable aid to Grandpop both in the construction of the "Bonnie Belle" and in being first mate on fishing trips. According to family members, Harvey rode a billy goat to school, located about a mile up the road from the home. He would tether "Ole Bill" in the school yard and crawl in. He was always self-conscious and shy about his condition, but when he got to know people and was around them long enough his shyness was not as

Harvey Doxey Stowe

evident. His contemporaries were accustomed to seeing him crawl and ride his goat, with hardly passing notice. But to strangers who had never seen a person in this condition it was quite a shock.

Aunt Agnes Scarborough of Avon tells the story of the time when Grandma Millie, grandpop's mother who lived with him and grandmom Janette and was blind, one morning asked Janette where her breakfast was. "Why, it's right there in front of you," Janette explained. Grandma Millie said she couldn't find her breakfast and asked Janette if she was sure she had fixed it. About that time one of the children came in from the back yard and said "Ole Bill" had wandered in the back door where someone had left it cracked, and had stolen Grandmom Millie's breakfast and eaten it. "No wonder I couldn't find it," said Grandmom Millie. Not long after that "Ole Bill" died and all the children gathered for his funeral. They found a nice spot nestled in the live oaks and water myrtles between the house and landing and gave him an appropriate funeral.

    Shortly thereafter Grandpop secured a Model T Ford for Harvey, and he got his first taste of the operation of an automobile and the maintenance and upkeep of same. Needless to say he became a master mechanic out of necessity. He could do anything with his hands -- carpentry, cabinet-making, saw filer, and in later years he took up carving wooden ducks and geese which he sold to tourists, using his cousin Roland Stowe's White Cane Gift Shop as an outlet. Roland would take the crafts on consignment. Harvey helped Roland with his looms and separating various colored rags used in rug-making.

    Harvey graduated from the Model-T to a Model A sedan. He decided he wanted to make a pickup truck out of her, so he stripped the back end down to a flat bottom, built a truck-type body, and accomplished his purpose. That Model A had one failing -- she had to be jacked up from the rear, clearing the wheels so she could be cranked in gear. After getting her started we'd push her off the jack and take off! Harvey would always promise my brother and me a ride up the road if we would help get the car started. We'd jack her up. I'd go around front and crank until she started. Then we'd push her off, Harvey would give her full throttle and off he'd go in a cloud of dust without my brother and me, looking over his shoulder and saying he'd be back later. Often times while cranking, the engine would backfire, causing the crank to reverse itself and more than likely bringing on a broken arm. I was fortunate this never happened to me. Automobiles and equipment were referred to the same as a boat, using the pronouns "she" and "her".

In recent years we would mail Christmas gifts to Uncle Harvey. On a visit shortly after one of these holidays he inquired why the heck we sent him a funnel for Christmas? I looked at him questioningly. He continued, "I know I drink a little likker now and then, but I sure as h--- don't need a funnel to get it down!" He showed me the funnel, made from plastic and folded in the middle. It then dawned on me that in getting paper to stuff around the presents a funnel had fallen into the box containing old newspapers and excelsior used for packing, and I had unknowingly packed it with the presents. Henry Rumley had always been most generous in providing me with wrapping paper and gummed labels for the mailing. The next time I went by Rumley Motor Supplies I told Henry that I owed him for one plastic funnel. He wanted to know why, and when I related what had happened he almost died laughing and said the story was good enough to warrant gift of the funnel. From then on, every time I came back from a visit to Hatteras, Henry would ask me if I took Uncle Harvey a funnel.

UNCLE PRESTON

Uncle Preston Stowe served in the Lifesaving Service and later with the Lighthouse Service aboard the Diamond Shoals Lightship. Periodically the lightship would have to go on the ways at Norfolk for overhaul and repair. It was during these times that huge barnacles, some the size of conchs, would be scraped from the bottom.

Grandpop Irv works on his son Preston's boat, the "Miss Yvonne", while Lee Robinson, right, looks on. She was built in the hangar of the Gooseville Gun Club circa 1939.

They had the pretty color and hues of seashells found along the beaches. Members of the lightship crew would polish them, glue felt pads on the bottom, and sell them as souvenir ash trays. Uncle Preston and other crew members picked up a little extra cash with this hobby. After serving in the Lighthouse Service, Preston helped grandpop Irv in the construction of his fishing boat, the "Miss Yvonne", named for his youngest daughter. She was built in the Gooseville Gun Club's hangar and launched in "the canal", located a short distance away on the soundside. Preston and his son, William, fished and shrimped for a living, as did many other Hatteras families. In later years Uncle Preston and Uncle Harvey got into carving ducks and geese and mounting them on driftwood pedestals or from strings to be sold to the tourist trade. They had a perfect outlet for their handicraft in that Roland Stowe, a cousin who was legally blind, operated a White Cane Gift Shop in the lower part of Hatteras Village. He allowed Harvey and Preston to place their work in his shop on consignment. Harvey would help Roland in cutting and sorting materials used in rug weaving. When fishing fell off as a way of making a living and upon the advent of the paved highway, more tourists began to visit the villages of the Outer Banks and would pay good money for these native handicrafts.

PART THREE

CHAPTER ONE

ICE HOUSES

Prior to the construction of the harbor at Hatteras, "ice houses", or "wharves" were located out from shoreside to navigable depths for the fishing and freight boats. These "ice houses" were usually known by the owner's name and called thusly: "Mr. John Meekins" wharf" or "Mr. Rance Oden's wharf" or "Dolph Burrus' wharf" or "Irish Willis' wharf, and so on. They were called "ice houses" because this is where the ice was stored in 300-pound blocks that had been brought by the freight boats from Washington and Elizabeth City. Ice was used to preserve the boxes of fish being shipped out to the mainland. Before power operated machines came into being, hand-held chippers were used to shave the ice from the blocks. During the hot summer days we young'uns delighted in getting chunks of cooling ice. The ice houses and wharves also served as a mooring place for boats, although many owners preferred to keep their boats tied to a stake located a short distance from the shore in five or six feet of water.

Ice House - Frazier Peele, left, along with two other workers at Peele's ice house on the Hatteras waterfront, weigh and ice fish for shipment to Engelhard. Circa 1947. (Photo Courtesy N. C. Dep't Archives & History)

Mr. Rance Oden was the Gulf Oil dealer and also sold caskets for funerals. His home was located near his wharf and the casket house was just off the road behind the picket fence surrounding the property. We kids always gave the casket house a wide berth and quickened our pace when passing by on dark nights. Mr. Rance and the Willis brothers, S. P. and Pete, owners of S. P. Willis Fish House in Washington, had an interest in the "Mary Fletcher" which brought gasoline, oil and provisions each week. Mr. Rance's wife, Julia, was a school teacher and taught at least three generations of Hatteras children.

Rance Oden on the walkway of his home in Hatteras Village circa 1937 (Photo Courtesy N. C. Division of Archives and History)

Young and old alike gather at the Hatteras Post Office for the arrival of the mail truck circa 1947. Mr. Irish Willis' Grocery Store is in the background. (Photo Courtesy N.C. Dep't of Archives & History)

Mr. John Meekins, next-door neighbor to Irv and Janette Stowe, ran a general store just across from the "down-the-road" Methodist Church and just a clam shell's throw from where my grandparents lived. Many of his provisions arrived on the "Mary Fletcher" and "Flossie Muir".

Mr. Andrew (Ander) Austin ran a mercantile business on the main road coming into Hatteras and operated the only movie house on the island. Other merchants in the 1930's and early 40's included Mr. Reuben Ballance, Mr. Irish Willis, Mr. Dolph Burrus, Mr. Roscoe Burrus, and Mr. Dan Oden. Loren Ballance operated the pool room located in the middle of the village adjacent to the school yard. Lee Robinson retired from fishing and bought the property formerly belonging to Mr. John Meekins and operated a general store which later became one of the first supermarkets in the village. Millard Stowe, a newphew of

Mary M. Akers, nee Styron, in a 1947 photo, is shown leaving the Hatteras schoolhouse where she taught for several years. (Photo Courtesy N. C. Dep't Archives & History)

Grandpop Irv, had a neighborhood grocery located in what was an old kitchen to the rear of his home adjacent to the "down-the-road" Methodist Church. Mr. Ben Austin also had a neighborhood store. Frederick McCarthy and his wife, Mary Styron McCarthy, operated a grocery store following World War II. Mary also taught school. Harold Gray, brother of Mr. Damon Gray, operated a grocery and gas business. Mr. Damon was a barber and cultivated his hobby of wood carving at the same time. His barber shop was a favorite hangout for the men, and some tall tales were told, to be sure.

In addition to the movie and pool hall, other entertainment spots included the pavilion near the Atlantic View Hotel on the

Main intersection of Hatteras Village, 1939, as seen from porch of Dolph Burrus' store. Behind auto to right is Loren Ballance's pool hall and gas station, the schoolhouse and Methodist Church. Left background is the mercantile business of Ander Austin. (Photo Courtesy N. C. Dep't Archives & History)

beach coming into the village from the North, owned by Mr. Ellsworth Ballance, and The Beacon, a dance hall and night spot located on the other side of the road from the beach pavillion, owned by Willie Newsome. Buxton had its "Bloody Bucket" nightspot, the name coming, no doubt, from some of the "free-for-all" fights that were said to occur from time to time. Bootleggers plied their trade by selling half-pints and pints of "white lightnin'" that came from across the sound at East Lake on the Tyrrell County mainland. When this would run out those who imbibed would drink rubbing alcohol, bay rum, alcohol strained from cans of Sterno, or anything they could get their hands on that contained spirits -- even lemon extract!

At times overindulgence in spirits would bring on arguments which would lead to a "free-for-all" fight, and many times people would end up with various injuries that included black eyes and cuts from knives being wielded by the combatants.

Dolph Burrus is shown sweeping the porch of his mercantile business located at the main crossroad in Hatteras Village, circa 1939. (Photo courtesy N.C. Dep't Archives & History)

LAW ENFORCEMENT

There were no law enforcement officers stationed at Hatteras until some time after World War II, so the people more-or-less took care of matters in their own way. More serious offenses would call for a deputy to come down from Manteo. Some thought the Ku Klux Klan was the vehicle by which law and order was enforced. At any rate, if anyone was known to be getting out of hand with mean tricks, stealing, getting too drunk, fighting, or running around with another's wife, the word would go out. I have often heard it said a "secret meeting" was being held at a certain place up the road in which matters were being discussed dealing with the behavior of some of the islanders.

The soundside behind my grandparent's home was known as "the landing" where grandpop had a net house, net scaffolds, and where he kept his skiff which was used for getting out to where the "Bonnie Belle" was tied to her stake in deeper water. My childhood buddy Eldon Gaskins and I were coming home from swimming at the landing one day. It was a quiet, lazy afternoon in July and we were tired and hungry after a couple of hours of being in the salt water. We went into the house to get us a cold biscuit and anything else we could find to eat when a person in a white robe with a hood pulled over their head appeared at the head of the stairs with hands raised as if to swoop down on us! I forgot my hunger and so did Eldon.

We ran hard for his home where we hoped it would be safer than my house where that robed figure had scared us out of a year's growth! I never knew whether it was my grandfather trying to scare us, or my Aunt Mable, who had been known to pull a trick like that on occasion. Suffice it to say I always tried to steer clear of trouble while at Hatteras because I didn't want to come in contact with the "Ku Klux"!

CHAPTER TWO

LEGENDARY TOM ANGELL

When discussing the Oliver's Reef Lighthouse I am reminded of Tom Angell, who was the only black person living on Hatteras Island when I was growing up. According to an article written by Lou Angell and appearing in The State Magazine, June, 1981, Tom's original name was Thomas Vince, born in New Bern in 1865. Nelson Paul Angell and his wife, Inez arrived in the summer of 1874 to be the keeper of the new lighthouse at Oliver's Reef, and they brought young Tom with them to be their housekeeper and cook. It was said that Tom was the son of slave parents. Nelson Paul Angell built a magnificent home at Hatteras. Tom grew to be an accepted and respected member of the community, becoming one of the legends of the Outer Banks. The Angells were a prominent family with connections in New Bern. Theresa Shipp, former Register of Deeds of Craven County, now deceased, was related to the Angells on her mother's side of the family and spent summer vacations at Hatteras.

Nelson Paul Angell died in July, 1887 after serving 13 years as keeper of the Oliver's Reef lighthouse. Inez Angell died in 1912 and made Tom Angell the sole beneficiary of her estate. Tom inherited the land and house with all furnishings, and opened the home to everyone. It became a gathering point, especially on Sunday afternoons during the summer. When I spent summers at Hatteras with my grandparents in the 1930's, villagers would stroll down to Tom's for a Sunday outing. The children would play croquet and tag. There was an archery set for those who enjoyed shooting arrows at a target. The adults took to the swings and

77

easy chairs to pass a pleasant afternoon before having to get back home for supper and Sunday evening prayer meeting.

Tom would hire three or four of us youngsters to turn the cranks on his ice cream freezers. Our pay was one delicious dish of Tom Angell's special recipe. He usually turned out one freezer of chocolate, one of vanilla, and everybody's favorite, pineapple. Immaculate in his starched and ironed white ducks and jacket, Tom would serve from the gazebo (or pavilion) in his always neatly-kept yard. During cold, bleak winter days when the men didn't have much else to do, they were always welcome at Tom Angell's home to pass away the time swapping yarns and whittling away on a piece of wood.

Tom Angell was like a lot of other villagers who did whatever they could to earn enough to clothe and feed themselves and their families. Life was much tougher in those times than now. Tom fished on shares, raised chickens which he sold for whatever he could get for them, and did baking for regular customers. He would rent a room to drummers coming into the area and wanting to spend the night.

The Gooseville Gun Club played an important part in Tom's life. It was organized by a group from the north with Albert Lyon, Sr., from Detroit, as the chief stockholder. It was said that Mr. Lyon invented the automobile bumper, wheel covers and other automotive innovations. Mr. Lyon and his friends agreed to hire Tom Angell as their cook and this proved to be his chief means of upkeep until he died. When Tom developed cancer all his medical expenses were taken care of by the gun club members. They hired someone to look after him in his home when he was not able to care for himself and when he died they took care of his funeral expenses and erected an appropriate marker at his grave in the Angell cemetery located on the property at Hatteras.

One thing that always remained in my memory from my visits in Tom's home was the bronzed baby shoes on a table just inside the front door, the fine china stored in the china closet of the dining room, and other mementos preserved by Mrs. Angell of Tom's early childhood.

Although Tom was an accepted member of an all-white community and was loved by all, he will probably be remembered more for his Sunday afternoon ice cream socials than anything else. There's no debate that Tom Angell belongs to the heritage that is the story of Hatteras in our time. After Tom's death in 1937 the property reverted to the Angell estate and was sold. The home burned in 1945 and a modern home replaced it.

CHAPTER III

DAVE DRISCOLL, PILOT

Dave Driscoll was the pilot for Mr. Lyon and members of the Gooseville Gun Club which was located at a point between Ben's Creek and Goose Creek and is now the site of the Hatteras Inlet Coast Guard Station which was moved from the northern end of Ocracoke Island in the late 1940's due to erosion of the beach and a new inlet which cut through the site of the old Coast Guard station by a September storm.

Like Tom Angell, Dave Driscoll was a living legend of the Outer Banks during the 1930's. We young'uns would hear the drone of his aircraft and shout, "Here comes Dave Driscoll!" He'd dip his wings to us, circle around the p'int of beach at Hatteras Inlet, come back up into the wind, and land near the hangar located adjacent to the gun club.

Mr. Lon Neal, who lived up the road a short distance from my grandparents, was caretaker of the gun club. He had a speech impediment, and every time we kids would get close to the boundary line of the club property, Mr. Lon would come out with his .22 rifle, point it toward us, and holler out, "get vee off of vee c'ub house land, or vee will shoot vee in vee ass!" We got the message!

SOUP BOWL HAIRCUT

Mr. Rube Stowe, a nephew of my Grandpop Irv, lived just down the road and barbered on the side when he wasn't out in Pamlico Sound tending to his nets. I had gone for about two months without a haircut and Uncle Harvey told me I was going to have to pay "dog tax" if I waited much longer to get shorn. My hair always turned a flaxen yellow (almost white) when bleached by the summer sun and salt water. (I learned to swim at the age of five when Uncle Berry threw me in over my head and shouted, "Now, dammit, swim or drown!" I chose to swim!)

Mr. Rube was down to Core Sound on a fishing trip and wasn't available to cut my hair. Harvey told me that if Miss Fannie (Rube's wife) would let him borrow Mr. Rube's clippers and scissors, he'd cut my hair. Harvey sat me on a slop jar turned upside down on the back porch and proceeded to cut away, straight up the sides, back and front of my head.

I got what some called in those days a "soup bowl" or "pee-pot" haircut, scalloped and all. I resembled Moe of "The Three Stooges!" Harvey claimed 'twas 'cause I wouldn't sit still. I counterclaimed 'twas 'cause he didn't know the first darn thing about barbering!

THE GASKINS BOYS

The Gaskins boys will always live in my memory because their mother, Miss Rosa, fed me most of the time along with her four sons and husband. She'd cook three meals a day. I spent most of my waking hours playing with Eldon, who was my age, and Ben, a year or so younger. Keith was the baby and had his own friends, while Walton was oldest and his friends were three or four years older than us.

Mr. Ebby, the father, was usually busy tending his pound nets out in the sound, or mending nets at his camp up the road.

Miss Rosa made her boys read the Bible and they knew enough that Nebuchadnezzar was the King of Jews around 600 BC. When someone would ask one of the boys who his daddy was they had a stock answer. They'd say, "Why, he's Ebby-ka-needer, King of the Jews!"

Mending nets shoreside Hatteras Village, 1947. Fishing boat hauled up on shore for painting and repairs. Camp, homes in background. (Photo Courtesy N. C. Dep=t Archives and History).

Walton and several of his friends, including my Uncle Berry, were swimming at the beach one day when Walton saw what he thought was a glass float (used at that time on many nets) beyond the off-reef. He swam out to retrieve it and found quickly it was a Portugese Man-O-War, a deadly balloon-like creature with fiery tentacles extending from its "sail". Walton's body was engulfed in those tentacles and he was going under for the third time when two of the fellows finally got to him, pulled him ashore, administered first aid and resuscitation, bringing him around to a point where they could carry him to his home which was nearby. Dr. Kenfield administered medicines which brought him out of it, and he finally got well. Walton said he'd never let his curiosity get the best of him again in any such situation!

CHAPTER FOUR

MAKING A LIVING

In many parts of the country during the Great Depression of the 1930's people were having difficulty getting enough to eat. We heard and read of "soup lines" in the large cities and industrial centers. This was not as evident in this part of the country. Although my grandfather was captain of a freight boat that ran from Hatteras to Elizabeth City, he was not a wealthy man, but he usually brought home fresh meat and vegetables to feed a large family which included, at the time, a niece and nephew who lived with my grandparents. More often than not weekday meals consisted of bread and coffee for breakfast, boiled beans and baked beans for dinner and supper, along with more of those delicious hot biscuits cooked as only my grandmother could! On occasion there'd be molasses or syrup to sop the biscuits. Grandpop would buy flour by the barrel and pure lard by the 50-pound stand. When you're feeding a large family with hefty appetites, you buy groceries in wholesale lots. Grandmother was an expert at cooking those seven and nine-layer chocolate cakes, and her lace cornbread cooked in an iron frying pan defied description.

One could always get a mess of fish during the week by going up to the "ice house" (fish house) when the pound netters were coming in and helping to sort fish in the baskets, laying aside a mess for your own dinner. We'd clean and filet them and have fish two or three times a week. This fare could be augmented with a mess of clams, salt mullet, mullet livers and gizzards, soft crabs caught along the shoreside -- and always grandmother had enough dry beans on hand to assure that all hands would keep their bellies full. Occasionally Grandpop would bring home a large drum, filet and salt it down, and hang the pieces on wooden pegs to dry in the sun. My grandmother who I always called Nana, would later soak this salt fish, boil it in the pot, fry out grease from cracklin's which was poured over the delicious fish. To complete the menu she'd have boiled potatoes, sliced onions, and her famous fried lace cornbread.

Grandpop would take me "outside" fishing when the weather was good. The fishing grounds were located between Hatteras Inlet and Diamond Shoals. With Uncle Harvey at the helm, Grandpop would stand on the bow of the "Bonnie Belle", holding himself with a line tied to the forward pawl post, legs spread apart, smelling the air. He could actually sniff out a school of fish! The smell of the air changed from salt to "fresh" whenever a school was upwind of the boat, and a slick on the water usually indicated the presence of paydirt for the fisherman. The nets were coiled in a stern compartment with a staff attached to both ends. When fish were detected, the staff would be thrown over the stern with the net paying out in an arc around the school. When the corks would bob you knew fish were striking and hanging in the meshes. After setting for a sufficient length of time the nets would be hauled back into the compartment. One man would take the cork line and another the lead line, picking fish out and tossing them into a compartment midship. Croaker, trout, butterfish, sunfish, porgies, mackerel -- these were some of the varieties caught. They would be sorted and thrown into wire baskets and weighed upon arrival at the ice house. Wooden boxes were used to ice the fish down for shipment to terminals at Washington, Elizabeth City and Engelhard where they would be further sorted and processed for shipment to Norfolk and other northern markets. Croaker, butterfish and sunfish would bring about three cents a pound, while trout, bluefish, mackerel, and porgies would bring from five to six cents a pound, depending on how the market demand was on a particular day. There was always considerable activity around the ice houses when the fishermen would come in with their catch, and the seagulls would screech and fight over the discarded scraps. I've often heard Grandpop remark, "Well, young'uns, we didn't catch enough today to pay the gas bill".

One of the many jobs for the womenfolk around the house was to tie and mend nets. This consisted of purchasing the correct size net twine, winding the twine on a net needle, getting the correct sized mesh guage on which the loops were tied, and going to work. The young'uns would hold the skeins of twine on their arms while another would wind it on the needles, keeping a good supply ahead for the adults who were tying net. Each section would measure anywhere from 50 to 150 yards. This work usually was done inside the house during winter months.

The finishing touch was when the nets were tied to the cork and lead lines. Mending was done outside on a spread. Larger fish such as sharks and stingrays would tear large holes in the nets, or hard crabs would claw their way through when becoming entangled. These holes were closed by tying in to a corner of the torn-out section and estimating the mesh size, tying from one section to another.

Nets were preserved by dipping in lime water before hanging out on scaffolding to dry. There were set nets, drift nets, haul nets, mullet nets, shad nets, sink nets, and others, with each having a different mesh size. Natives referred to mesh as "marsh".

In later years monofilament nets of synthetic materials took over, eliminating the necessity of tying.

Pound nets were tarred in huge pots located on the shoreside. This was man's work. The fresh smell of molten tar would permeate the air after one of these sessions as the nets were spread on scaffolds to dry.

A pound net is like a huge cage where the lead net directs the fish through a trap into the impoundment. They can be left in place over a long period of time. They are fished by lifting the sides and using a dip net to remove the catch.

Mr. Lee Robinson was one of the foremost pound netters and often would let us accompany him to his nets. We'd leave out of the Canal where he kept his shad boat. The Canal was a dredged-out creek leading up to the Gooseville Gun Club, and site of the N. C. Ferry Dock today. We'd get underway around 4:00 A. M. and get out to the nets around daybreak. It would usually take from 30 to 40 minutes to fish the pound, and on the way to the ice house we would sort the fish and be ready to weigh in upon arrival at the dock.

We caught a large sea turtle (called "terkle" by Outer-Bankers) one day. Mr. Lee threw the critter up on the dock and after weighing in and getting his tickets, he dressed the "terkle" and distributed the meat to people in the neighborhood who loved stewed turtle and turtle soup. One amazing phenomenon that always intrigued me was the fact that a sea turtle's heart, when removed, keeps beating until the sun goes down.

There were times when the market would be depressed and fishermen would have to dump their catch when they did not have ice to keep them until the market could recover. If Grandpop heard of the market being depressed he would stay home. Uncle Harvey, in addition to being the helmsman, was also chief cook and bottle washer. He didn't have to cook much because we mostly ate canned beans, vienna sausage, potted meat and soda crackers. I drank water while Uncle Harvey and Grandpop usually had something a little stronger!

We were haul netting at Hatteras Inlet one day and had made a good catch of spot. Harvey cleaned a mess for our dinner but found there was no lard with which to fry them, so he put them in a tea kettle and turned the fire up and let them boil in salt water dipped from the sound. We got busy and forgot about the fish until Harvey, who was famished, remembered and went below to turn off the fire. The fish had boiled to pieces. Harvey poured them from the spout, drained off the water, and we had boiled spot along with cold biscuits left over from the day before. Anything and everything tastes good when you're working around salt water!

Mr. Fred Stowe, a nephew of Grandpop Irv, and his boys, Frederick, Charles, Lewis and Elmo, were known far and wide along the Outer Banks for their expertise in mulleting, which required plenty of organization and hard work. Mr. Fred's camp (a net house was referred to as a camp) was located on property adjacent to Grandpop's landing. He kept his skiffs tied off about 100 feet from shoreside.

When the mullet were running, Mr. Fred and his boys would fish all night, getting in with their catch around daylight.

The skiffs would be pulled as close to shore as possible and wooden barrels and bags of salt would be in place to receive the mullets when cleaned and split open. These were the famous Hatteras salt mullets, known equally as well as the familiar Ocracoke salt mullets! As many as 12 to 15 people would work furiously to split the fish, take out the innards, but save the livers and gizzards, considered by many as a delicacy. Schools of small fry always found close to shore, hard crabs, and the ever-present seagulls, would feast on the scraps. Those helping out would set aside a mess of mullet, along with livers and gizzards if they fancied them, and this would be dinner for that day.

Charles served in the U. S. Coast Guard and while stationed at Ocracoke in the 1950's, he played guitar in a band with some of the other crewmen. He was a very proficient musician, and one of his favorites was "Charlie Mason Pogie Boat". I had heard of "The Wreck of The Charlie Mason" and asked Charles to sing it for me when the Coast Guard picket boat was docked at the Washington Buoy Yard during a waterfront event in the '50's. Though I have long forgotten the words, I recently visited the North Carolina Maritime Museum at Beaufort, N. C., and met Connie Mason, Collections Manager for the museum who herself is a songwriter and published a collection of her songs which are native to the Morehead City and Beaufort area. In the course of conversation with her we mentioned Charles and "Wreck of the Charlie Mason," and she remembered having heard it and had even sung it with a group. She was kind enough to send me a copy of the words to "Charlie Mason Pogie Boat".

Charlie Mason Pogie Boat

It was the First of January in the New Year '48,
While fishing off the loopshack Charlie Mason met her fate.
It was a pretty day that morning, with a light southerdly wind,
In the evening it looked different,
The Cap thought he should come in.

He gave orders to pick up port boat, and the starboard too,
When the falls broke on the starboard side
And the net went in the screw.
Now, Wiley called the Coast Guard. NAN AMC NAN 2 9
Send your 83 footer and your best piece of line.

The crew they manned the patrol boat immediately left the station,
Proceeded through the inlet, up to the Charlie Mason.
They got the line made fast when the bit broke like a match,
Then Wiley knew he lost his boat, and all of his catch.

I'm coming ashore Coast Guard, you better make a start,
Then the crew of the Coast Guard station
Broke out their old beach cart.
They backed up the bomb service for the beach cart to hook,
There was nothing but Core Sounders anywhere you might look.

And then Vann Henry said "Stanley hear my plan,
Harvey Smith says he'll pay us thirty grand,
He'll pay that sum if we can float,
That Charlie Mason Pogie boat.

Now Lum he said to William, you load the old Lyle gun,
When he went to pull the lanyard you could see the
  fellows run,
The Lyle gun she wouldn't fire, it was an awful disgrace,
Lum couldn't see a blessed thing, his hat blew in his face.

But they finally got the hawser out and tied it to the mast,
They stepped the crotch and fixed the buoy,
The thing was rigged at last.
First man crawled in the buoy, the crew they heaved
  around,
He was so heavy the hawser sagged, poor devil nearly
  drowned

Now all the men were saved that night
All except'n one, this man he had a heart attack.
His name was Payton Young,
Ansley O'Neal brought him over to the Coast Guard
  station,
The crew they worked him over on artificial respiration.

But then Henry said, Stanley hear my plan
Harvey Smith says he'll pay us thirty grand
He'll pay that sum if we can float,
That Charlie Mason Pogie boat.

Up at Travis Williams's you could hear this conversation,
If I had the equipment, I'd float that Charlie Mason.
But Stanley Wahab told his men, you float that craft for me
And Sunday the Fourth of April she was in Beaufort, N. C.

PARADOX

In recent years I have been dismayed by the large number of signs located at various points between Hatteras village and the inlet admonishing, "Do not take shellfish from this area: waters polluted". Of course, all one has to do is take a look around and see where a harbor has been dredged as the site of a marina, the State Ferry docks are adjacent with ferries running constantly, and state dredges dump spoil in areas between the ferry landing and the inlet. This spoil spreads out, disturbing the ecological balance of the area, and thus makes it unfit for taking shellfish and more than likely spoiling the area for the taking of other marine life. This is an interesting paradox. On the one hand we're furnishing services for a large number of people, and on the other we're denying the taking of resources from public waters because of pollution.

SPORT FISHING

When commercial fishing faded as a way of making a living, old timers who had survived from this endeavor began to outfit their boats for sports fishing and a new industry was born. Bookings were made with parties from far and near. Some of the first to transfer from commercial to sportsfishing were the Foster brothers, Ernal, Hallis, Bill and Gaston, sons of Charlie and Sue Foster. Mr. Charlie owned the "Albatross" and this boat along with others acquired later constituted the "Albatross" fleet of sportsfishing boats operating out of Hatteras. Edgar Styron was also among the first, and he later captained large yachts owned by sportsmen from other places. Several of the younger generation of Hattersmen became pilots or captains for these outside owners, and the Blue Marlin Marina became an exclusive club for sportsfishermen.

The "Albatross I" of the Albatross fleet of sports fishing boats owned by the Foster family at Hatteras circa 1947. (Photo Courtesy N. C. Dep't Archives & History)

CHAPTER FIVE

TAKIN' IN WASHIN'

"Blue Monday" is bound to have gotten that designation because of being wash day in most households. In addition to her own, Nana would wash for some families who lived up the road to earn a little extra change. It was the job of youngsters to gather wood to keep the fire going under the boiling pot in the backyard. Some people used round, cast-iron pots for this purpose, but Nana used a 50-pound lard stand elevated on four bricks which got the job done just as well. A four-foot stick was used to stir the clothes, and when they were sufficiently boiled they would be wrapped around the stick and taken from the pot to be placed in the rinse water which was drawn from the cistern and placed in a large zinc tub. A portion of bluin' was added to whiten the sheets and white clothes. Nana made lye soap from grease drippings, Red Devil lye, and whatever other ingredients were required. An iron pot was used to mix the stuff, and this was cooked over an open fire in the back yard in the same pit used for the clothes boiling pot. It would then be poured into an old baking pan to cool and harden, then cut into blocks and placed on the wash bench on the back porch. This coarse lye soap was used for heavy-duty work clothes. Lighter fabrics were washed with the popular packaged soaps of that time. Octagon soap was the old standby for those who did not care to make their own. Nowadays tender hands would require the use of rubber gloves to keep from losing the skin, but back then Nana's hands were tough from using the scrub board and all the other chores expected of a mother and housewife.

(My first contact with Octagon soap was when I was five and uttered a couple of nasty words I had heard some of the older boys use while playing. It was at the dinner table -- we ate dinner in the middle of the day -- and my father, although he was familiar with the words, did not approve of a five-year-old using them at the table. Whereupon he went to the kitchen sink, got a half-used bar of Octagon, took out his pocket knife, peeled off a good-sized handful of chips, and proceeded to cram them in my mouth. "Now, chew 'em up, and let me never hear you use such vile language at the dinner table again," he admonished.)

The clothesline ran from the corner of the house, across the yard to a post at the corner of the chicken pound, thence to the "old kitchen", a room that had served as a kitchen before Grandpop re-modeled and built a new kitchen and dining room on the house, thence to the beginning. These lines would accommodate two or three big washings. With a fresh breeze always prevailing from the sou-west, it didn't take long for the clothes to dry. Then came the ironing chores in the afternoon. Before Nana got her new Florence kerosene cook stove, she owned a Southern Comfort wood and coal burning stove. The flat irons were placed on the top of this stove to be heated, and the detachable handles were used to keep switching when the irons would cool. Green cedar leaves or pine straw was used to rub the hot irons on to remove any smut and also to give the clothes a "fresh" smell. This was a hot task during summer months, but thanks to prevailing breezes drawing through the kitchen and dining room, heat from the stove was not unbearable.

Finally the finished basket piled high with fresh-smelling, starchy clothes with clean bath towels tucked in around the sides as a cover, would be ready to be delivered. My brother would take one handle and I the other, and we'd deliver to Nana's regular customers who sometimes would reward us with a nickel or dime. Ten cents would buy a large "Mr. Goodbar" and a Pepsi, which we shared.

EARN YOUR KEEP

My grandmother was a very frugal lady and insisted that I earn my keep on my summer visits. Grandpop rigged me a clam rake and made a small, wooden flat to put me in the clamming business. A clam rake had curved tines and chicken wire netting attached from the ends of the rake back to the handle. One would wade along pushing the rake ahead and upon striking a clam, get the curved tine under the mussel, dig it out of the sand, while at the same time swiftly turning the rake over to catch the clam on the wire netting. One would then turn, deposit the clam in the flat which was connected with the person by a small line and pulled behind, until it was full enough to wade back and deposit in the skiff. Upon arrival at the landing, we would throw the clams around a stake and they would bed themselves. An iron stake marked the site. My first cousin, Rudolph Peele, clammed with me and had a bed adjacent to mine. His father, Litchfield Peele, was caretaker of the Green Island Gun Club which was located about three miles south of Hatteras Inlet on Ocracoke Island and owned by a group of sportsmen from up North. Rudolph and I would spend two or three days at the Gun Club on occasion, and clam on the shoal in the inlet, a long, sandy spit pushed by the tidal currents going to and fro in the inlet. We'd bed them at the landing behind the gun club until we departed for Hatteras, then load them on the gasboat and take them home to be deposited in the beds behind our grandparents' home.

We'd also catch softcrabs along the shoreside, wading along and looking for the tell-tale shed where a softcrab would be lurking beneath a brick or some other object on the bottom. Mr. Ellsworth Ballance operated the Atlantic View Hotel and would pay us 25 cents a dozen for softcrabs and one cent each for clams. Some days we'd make as much as two or three dollars, depending on the demand from Mr. Ellsworth. Often we would have our own roast on the shoreside, building a fire, letting it die down to hot coals, and placing the crabs in wet seaweed, smolder them in the hot coals until steamed to perfection, and then eat until one popped! Some of Grandmom's cold biscuits and raw Irish potatoes completed the menu. We peeled the potatoes with our teeth. This was the Hatteras version of a New England Shore dinner!

Grandpop made me a special dip net for hard crabbing on Oliver's Reef and along the shoreside. We'd wade along in grassy bottom looking for the large blue channel crabs lurking in the area, and when a crab was spotted we would make a swooping motion with the dip net and bring in the crab, depositing it in the little wooden flat being pulled behind. When the flat was full, we'd transfer the crabs to a barrel in the skiff, and head out for more. When the barrels were full we'd head for the ice house where crabs were readied for shipment to factories at Engelhard and Belhaven where pickers removed the succulent meat and packed it in tins to be shipped to various outlets. We were paid 50 cents a barrel for hard crabs. We would receive a chit (ticket) with the amount due written on it, and on Saturday mornings we'd collect for our week's work, which most of the time would amount to a whopping $2.50 up to $5.00 -- and that, to us, was BIG money during the depression! Grandmom kept my money. She would dole out a few pennies now and then when I had taken care of any chores she had assigned, and when I had saved enough, she would get out one of her mail-order catalogues and proceed to order clothes for me to finish out the summer and start school in the fall upon my return to Washington.

Cousin Rudolph's family moved to Manteo just prior to World War II and after getting out of the service Rudolph went into the charter sports fishing business. Grandpop helped Rudolph build his first sports fishing boat, a 40-footer which was developed and took shape in his back yard. She was named the "Martha" after Rudolph and Maxine's daughter. Later he secured another boat for taking fishing parties out from the Oregon Inlet Sports Fishing Center. He retired in 1992 after a long career. It followed naturally that Rudolph's son, Wesley, took up crabbing at an early age, having his own crab pots and impoundments for keeping "peelers" until they emerged as soft crabs. A ready market was available at the many motels and restaurants along the beaches of Nags Head and Kill Devil Hills.

Rudolph's mother, Etta, practiced midwifery for a number of years, following in the footsteps of her mother and my grandmother Janette Stowe. Etta had a clinic consisting of two rooms at the rear of her home in Manteo, and would board mothers-to-be until their babies arrived. Women would come from as far away as Ocracoke and Corolla to have their babies at Aunt Etta's clinic.

Janette Stowe brought three generations of children into the world during her career as a midwife. Dr. John Kenfield practiced medicine at his Hatteras clinic and was on hand for most deliveries. Women would come from all points along the Outer Banks. They'd arrive in horse and buggy, sail skiff or gas boat before automobiles came. Many a night I have heard a voice call from the front porch, "Miss Janette, mom is ready and has sent me fer to get you." Nana had a small satchel containing her medicines and instruments. She always kept a small bottle of whiskey "just in case" the patient might need a "little extra". She would also mix whiskey with camphor sticks to make a rubbing balm.

She liked to tell the story of when a man came and knocked on her door one day and when she greeted him, he said, "you don't know me, do you?" She looked real careful and replied, "No, I don't know you." He then said, "Well, you brought me into the world 45 years ago today at Ocracoke and I made up my mind to come see you because today's my birthday!"

She said the reason so many babies were named for her was because when the parents couldn't pay for her services, she'd just say, "name the child for me, and that's pay enough." In a television interview she was asked about how she got paid, and she told them that a lot of times people would give her a mess of collards and say 'thanks' and that would be enough. The television announcer said that if anyone inquires around Hatteras about Mrs. Stowe, the midwife, you ask for Miss Janette, Aunt Janette, or Cousin Janette. She answered to all these names, and as the case usually is in a small place, just about everyone is related to everyone else. She told about a man and woman from New Bern coming to see her as a result of the television interview.

Nana liked to tell of her younger years and of how her family and her marriage were important. She'd tell about the old Southern Comfort range that she cooked on for her large family. The wood for firing the cook stove was brought over from Hyde County by grandpop Irv because they didn't want to chop down the trees around the property. Later, the old Southern Comfort was replaced by a new, modern Florence oil stove, and in the 1950's a gas stove was installed with gas piped in from a tank outside the kitchen window.

Janette was a good story-teller, and she was written up in the Cape Hatteras School publication of "The Sea Chest" which used many of her stories.

Janette Stowe joins other legendary figures of the Outer Banks, delivering or assisting in the delivery of more than 350 babies, many of whom bear her name to this day. She was the subject of feature articles appearing in several North Carolina and Virginia newspapers. She lived to within two months of being 100, born in 1883, died in 1983.

Dr. John Kenfield, a legendary figure, was a chain smoker, always having a cigarette hanging from his lips, causing his upper lip to be stained yellow from nicotine. He peered over his glasses when he spoke. He owned a nice home located on the "slash" just behind what is now the Methodist parsonage. The "Slash" is a creek that traverses Hatteras Village from the bay to the north, meandering through the middle of town where the "Slash Bridge" allows traffic over the main road, southward to where it crosses the road in the southern part of the village, and on out into the sound just north of the site of a marina.

Janette Stowe (1883-1983)

PART FOUR

CHAPTER ONE

*THE PILOT OF HATTERAS

(From the National Gazette, Philadelphia,
Monday, January 16, 1792)

In fathoms five, the anchor gone,
While here we furl the sail,
No longer vainly laboring on
Against the Western gale;
While here thy bare and barren cliffs,
O Hatteras, I survey,
And shallow grounds and broken reefs:
What shall amuse my stay?

The Pilot comes. From yonder sands
He shoves his barque so frail,
And hurrying on, with busy hands,
Employs both oar and sail.
Beneath this rude, unsettled sky
Condemn'd to pass his years;
No other shores delight his eye,
No foe alarms his fears.

In depths of woods his hut he builds,
Where ocean around him flows,
And blooming in the barren wilds
His simple garden grows.

His wedded nymph, of sallow hue,
No mingled colors grace.
For her he toils, to her is true,
The captive of her face.

Kind nature here, to make him blest,
No quiet harbor plann'd,
And poverty, his constant guest,
Restrains the pirate band.
His hopes are all in yonder flock
Or some few hives of bees,
Except, when bound for Ocracock,**
Some gliding barque he sees;

His Marian then he quits with grief,
And spreads his tottering sails.
While, waving high her handkerchief,
Her commodore she hails.
She grieves, and fears to see no more
The sail that now forsakes,
From Hatteras' sands to banks of Core,
Such tedious journeys takes.

Fond nymph! your sighs are breath'd in vain,
Restrain those idle fears,
Can you, that should relieve his pain,
Thus kill him with your tears?
Can absence thus beget regard,
Or does it only seem?
He comes to meet a wandering band

That seeks fair Ashley's stream.
Tho' disappointed in his views,
Not joyless will we part;
Nor shall the god of mirth refuse
The balsam of the heart.
No niggard key shall lock up joy;
I'll give him half my store,
Will he but half his skill employ
To guard us from your shore.

Where western gales once more awake
What dangers will be near,
Alas! I see the billows break,
Alas! why came I here?
With quarts of rum and pints of gin,
Go, pilot, seek the land,
And drink till you and all your kin
Can neither sit nor stand.

SINBAD

*Written off the Cape, July, 1789, on a voyage to South Carolina, being detained sixteen days with strong gales ahead.

**All vessels from the northward that pass within Hatteras Shoals, bound for New Berne and other places on Pamlico Sound, commonly, in favorable weather, take a Hatteras pilot to conduct them over the dangerous bar of Ocracock, eleven leagues W. S. W. of the Cape.

[The above copied from "Reminiscenses & Memoirs of North

Carolina & Eminent North Carolinians" by Col. John Hill Wheeler of Hertford County, born 1808, died 1882, eminent military man and genealogist. Baltimore, Genealogical Publishing Co., 1966.]

SEPTEMBER STORMS

The 1938 September storm had brought the sea tide over the land and contaminated the ground water supply with salt, making it undrinkable and not fit for any use except washing clothes. The intrusion of salt water had turned the ground water supply to an amber color and this would yellow the clothing unless large amounts of clorox were used to bleach white goods, and too much clorox would weaken the fabric. Nana said other arrangements had to be made about getting water. The cistern was invaded by salt water. We had cleaned it using clorox and lysol to disinfect. We had to have drinking water as well as wash water. The tall sand dunes up the road in the area called "The Ridge" was where the fresh water supply was to be found. Pitcher pumps were located between the dunes and people lined up to fill whatever vessel they could find to hold water. Uncle Harvey had just converted his Model A Ford into a pickup by stripping the back end off and making a wooden flatbed just aft of the drivers' seat.

We had an old 50-gallon gas tank that had lain in the yard for a long time, plus all the wash tubs and buckets we could find. We loaded the Model A, took off for the Ridge, and started pumping. After we had filled everything in sight with clear water, we headed back to the house. We always had to jack up the back end of that Model A before she could be cranked and started. As luck would have it, she stalled in a sandy rut of the road. We had to unload the water, jack her up, get her started, reload the water, push her off the jack, and get her on the way again! We were completely exhausted when we got back home!

Every summer would bring a new crop of "wigglers" in the cistern. These are mosquito larvae. Nana used a tea strainer to separate the "wigglers" from the water. We occasionally swallowed a few when we didn't take time to strain them out. Prior to going in swimming each spring we would have to go to the Beaufort County Health Department where Miss Eva Cratt would innoculate us with typhoid shots, which were administered over a three-week period. The first shot would not be so bad and the second would cause some fever, but the third always left us with a high fever that lasted for a day. It evidently helped because the Pamlico River at that time received all the raw sewage from the Town of Washington, and Lord knows what else! And we had to combat the effect of the "wigglers" and mosquitoes at Hatteras. Some of the old-timers referred to the large mosquitoes as "New Jersey gallinippers!" When mosquitoes swarmed so thick they caused a "smoke" or cloud, we would get old rags, place them in a bucket and let them smolder, with the acrid smoke, hopefully, driving the mosquitoes away. Later, the spray truck would pass up and down the road emitting a vapor of DDT and other chemicals. This did not seem to have much effect on the pests, and in later years the procedure was outlawed because of adverse effects of the sprays on the environment. Nana always relied on her "fly tox" gun to spray for flies and mosquitoes in the house.

1944 HURRICANE

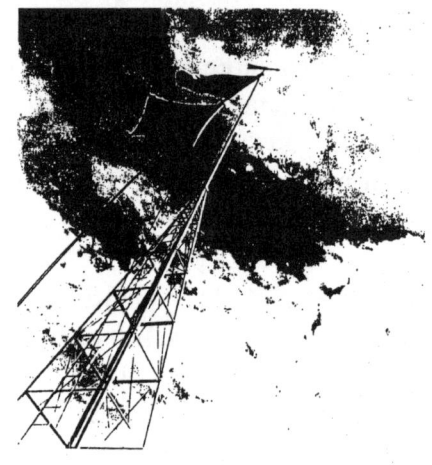

Hurricane warning flags fly from tower at Hatteras Signal Office announcing the September hurricane of 1944.

All day on the 13th of September, 1944, the radio had been crackling out warnings about an impending hurricane. Tropical storms had no names at this time. It was some years later that the National Hurricane Center began naming these depressions which were born in the south Atlantic and would move their way across the Caribbean and many times would assault the East Coast anywhere from Florida to the Virginia Capes and on up. The North Carolina coast has always been vulnerable because it juts so far out into the Atlantic and is close to the Gulf Stream, where many storms follow a path. Hatterasmen called these September storms "harricanes".

On the morning of September 14 at around 4:00 A. M. the wind began to freshen and whistle around the eaves. Grandpop and Harvey were across the sound shrimping and had taken refuge in Engelhard Creek to wait out the big storm. I was visiting with my grandmother between summer school and the fall quarter at UNC-CH. My aunt Mable and her five-year old son, Earl, were living there at the time. On the evening of the 13th we had placed all the furniture on blocks and battened down all that could be secured.

Nana sent me up the road to help Mrs. Lovie Burrus get her chickens in from where they had already gone to roost in the yaupon bushes in her yard. We had gotten all of them gathered with the exception of one old Dominicker hen who was clucking and fussing about being disturbed. She was roosting high in the yaupon, and I had just fixed my feet between two limbs and was reaching for her legs when I felt something warm and oozy hit me directly in the top of my head! That old Dominicker had turned loose a full load of her excrement, aimed, no doubt, at my face -- but I had just looked down to see about my footing when she decided to bombard me. I hollered for Miss Lovey and she almost died laughing before she got a wet cloth and helped clean me up! Her chickens went to roost on her kitchen cabinets that night!

When Nana roused me from a deep sleep at 4:00 A. M. on the 14th, the first thing she had me do was to chop off the head of a Rhode Island Red hen she had been saving for Sunday dinner. We cleaned the bird and placed the parts in the big stew pot. Later Nana would add pie bread and potatoes. "We'll at least not go hungry if this storm gets too bad," she said. By 8:00 A. M. the wind was blowing at near hurricane force from the sou-east, bringing the sea tide over the beach, coming down the sandy roads, and cutting under the house, on its way to meet the waters of the sound. Sea tide would undercut and wash out deep furrows, while the sound tide covered the land and inundated everything. Traveling counter-clockwise between 8:00 and 10:00 o'clock, the wind kept backing around more out of the west'ard, and it wasn't long before huge waves from the sound were rolling across the marsh between the house and the landing. The glass (barometer) continued to drop dangerously close to the 28.0 level and Nana kept giving it a little tap to make sure the indicator was correct. Mable and I didn't pay much attention to the barometer since we were busy shoring up doors and windows against the furious onslaught of the now huge waves coming in from the sound side and crashing up against the side of the house.

Some years earlier during a hurricane, Grandpop had cut a hole about six inches in diameter in the corner of the living room floor in order to let water into the house when the tide rose. When the sound tide began rising under the house around 9:30 A. M., the water began bubbling through the hole. The weight of the water helped hold the house on its blocks and foundation. We also left the back door open on the lee side to let water in from the back porch. Upon measuring the depth of the water inside the house we found it to be 18 inches and still rising between 10:15 and 11:00 A. M. The two-seater outdoor toilet was situated about 100 feet from the back porch toward the sound side. Nana saw it coming -- a huge wave tore it loose from over the pit, and it came barreling toward the house.

"H'its a-agoin' to hit us!" shouted Nana.

"Oh my Lord," moaned Mable.

"Help, save me!" cried Little Earl.

As fate would have it, the old toilet got snagged on two sturdy yaupons located just to the corner of the front porch, and it took a turn which carried it beyond the front porch and on its way toward the road in front of the house. It snagged on a fence post by the family graveyard, and after the tide went down it settled upside down in the middle of the road.

Meanwhile, a towering wave came rolling across the marsh from soundside and hit the back kitchen door with such force that it tore the door from its hinges. I secured a piece of 2 x 4 and some 10 penny nails, and with the help of Grandpops' hatchet which I had gotten from his tool box, I proceeded to nail the 2 x 4 across the errant door. I called for Nana, who had gone upstairs, to come and help me hold the door while I nailed the board. Every time a sea would surge against the door it would push me in with it and I was having difficulty getting a nail to hold in the door facing. Mable was busy attending to little Earl. Nana shouted back over the din of crashing waves and howling winds, "I can't come right now 'cause I'm up here stripped stark naked a-tryin' to get on a dry stitch of clothin'!" All of us were soaked. This was no time to fret over being wet. I finally managed to secure the weakened door and went on to nail a piece of plyboard over a window where two panes had blown out. We could feel a surge every time a wave would hit the house, thinking it would wash off the blocks at any minute. But the weight of the water which had been let in through the hole in the living room kept the house on its foundation, although later it was found that it had skewed about three inches causing some of the foundation blocks to tilt and the dining room floor to sag in the middle. The onslaught of waves and wind continued, and the house would shiver and shake, but it withstood all the sea and wind could dish out.

Little Earl was about half-way upstairs when he hollered down to his mother, "Mom, I've got to wee-wee!"

"Well, just take it out and wee-wee between the stair posts into the living room floor," his mother answered. Whereupon he took his mother at her word and let it go right in the middle of the living room floor, which by this time had about 22 inches of water on it anyhow!

While the hurricane was at its height we were sitting in middle bedroom upstairs enjoying stewed chicken, pie bread, boiled Irish 'taters, cold biscuits and iced tea. Every time a sea would crash against the side of the house, the ice would tinkle in the glass. Never did something to eat taste better than food did that day! We later learned the cups blew off the anemometer at the Weather Bureau (we called it the Signal Office) when the wind reached 85 mph, and some educated guesses were that the wind blew as hard as 125-130 mph. The double red hurricane warning flags were in tatters, but the flag pole remained intact. Between 1:00 and 2:00 P. M. the wind began to abate and patches of blue sky began to appear as angry, dark, scudding clouds began to dissipate and the tide to recede. "Get some brooms," shouted Nana, "and we'll sweep that water and muck right out the front door!" Some mucky residue was left by the receding waters but this was quickly removed. I secured a small zinc tub and bailed water from the back porch, swashing it down through the house toward the front door while Mable and little Earl helped with brooms, and Nana, with her trusted bottle of Lysol, began spraying that smelly disinfectant around. By the middle of the afternoon the winds had calmed and the tides receded, leaving considerable devastation and property damage.

Richard Dailey, keeper of the Hatteras Signal Office of the U. S.Weather Bureau, is shown adjusting the anemometer on the Signal Office tower at Hatteras Weather Bureau. During the 1944 hurricane the cups blew off the anemometer when the wind reached 125 mph. (Photo Courtesy N. C. Dep't Archives & History)

Hattersmen were accustomed to these storms. Although there were many broken windows and doors, missing shingles, a missing out-house, and considerable water damage, there was nothing insurmountable that could not be repaired. Several fishing boats moored offshore had dragged their anchors and washed up on the soundside, and automotive equipment suffered salt water damage. Uncle Harvey's car, parked adjacent to the house on the East side, suffered water damage. A well-known characteristic of Outer Bankers is that they always stick together during hard times, and with everyone pitching in and helping, things were soon set back in place and order restored. Some of the stronger boys in the neighborhood helped us lift the two-seater toilet, place it on the back of a pickup and set it back on a new pit we had dug in the vicinity of the old hole.

Two days later Grandpop and Harvey arrived from Engelhard. "Where were you all during the hurricane?" we asked. "Hoigh and droigh in Engelhard Creek," replied Grandpop. The west wind had pushed water out of Pamlico River and all the tributaries, leaving boats that had taken refuge lying on their sides. "I opened the hatch to check the weather," said Grandpop, "when all of a sudden I saw what I thought was the largest bird I'd ever seen a-flappin' its wings and headed for the marsh. I found out later it was the roof off a camp. The wind just lifted the whole roof off and it came sailin' through the air, resemblin' a great big bird!"

I remained through the weekend to help with the cleanup, and as there was no other way off the island Grandpop and Harvey transported me to Engelhard where I caught a ride with Max Mann on the mail truck back to Washington and eventually back to Chapel Hill where they had heard that I had been washed out to sea by the hurricane! Many hurricanes have hit the Outer Banks, since 1944 -- but this one will always live vividly in my memory, since I was there! In the 1950's Hurricanes Hazel and Barbara did considerable damage, and other storms during that time included Dianne, Ione and Connie. The Outer Banks area has been assaulted harder by Northeasters in recent years than by hurricanes, with large areas suffering erosion and damage to personal property.

The late Tom Spencer, erstwhile newsman of Engelhard who later was Managing Editor of The Washington Daily News and a close personal friend of this writer, was editor of the Hyde County Herald at the time of the 1944 hurricane and pointed out to his readers that the storm did extensive damage to crops and buildings. Farmers estimated crop losses at 75 per cent. Spencer wrote, "winds of gale proportions began blowing in the early hours of the morning and reached a peak about 10 o'clock. Residents had been warned that the hurricane was coming. D. L. Berry, chairman of the Hyde County Chapter of the American Red Cross, was notified to be on the alert with his organization. Radio stations carried the announcement in bulletins all day Wednesday. When the wind stopped blowing and the sun came out this afternoon crops were flat on the ground and farmers were estimating losses at 75 per cent. Fruit orchards were damaged throughout the county and the bean crop was said to be an almost total loss. The grape crop, already short, also suffered damage."

Continuing, Spencer wrote: "Mr. Barber of Currituck township, was reported missing. He left to go crabbing and at last reports today had not been found. A search was underway this afternoon to locate him. The county was cut off from the outside world except by private motor transportation. Telephone lines were down and it was impossible to reach points out of the county. Some local calls could be made but some of the circuits were not in working order. Electric power went off about 6:00 o'clock in the morning and remained off. Linemen of the Pamlico Ice and Light Company were able to get lights operating in the Town of Engelhard this evening. Damage to the power lines was extensive with numerous breaks in the miles of rural lines running to Swan Quarter, Fairfield and Manns Harbor.

"The Engelhard Bus Company did not operate either its Columbia or Washington routes today. Trees were blown across the highway on both sides of Swan Quarter hindering motor traffic. Some were able to get through, however, and this afternoon highway crews were clearing the path. The U. S. Mail truck came in from Washington. Rural mail carriers made their routes at Swan Quarter and Fairfield, but Mr. Fisher at Lake Landing and Mr. Watson at Scranton did not make theirs. Workstock was reported killed in Lake Landing and Currituck townships when barns and stables blew down. Details were not available. The Watson's Chapel Methodist Church at Nebraska was leveled by the wind. Another building reported blown down was the George L. Cox warehouse at Middletown located in front of his store. Reports coming in from the Swan Quarter section tell of a great deal of damage. The Methodist church was damaged to the tune of something like $100 and Soule church was damaged by a falling tree.

"Three chimneys were blown off the Fairfield school building. Details of other damage in that community were not available. At Engelhard, half of the new roof on J. H. Jarvis' store was ripped off and about two thirds of the roof on the Pamlico Ice and Light Company plant was blown off. (No doubt this was one of the roofs Grandpop Irv thought was a giant bird!) Numerous small houses were blown down or damaged. The storm, part of a great Atlantic hurricane that swept up from the South, was said by old timers to be one of the most severe to strike this section in recent years. No official word was available as to the rate of the wind, but some estimated it at 100 miles per hour. The hurricane reported heading in this direction yesterday was reported to be blowing 140 miles per hour. It is believed to be even more destructive than the one of 1933, which was one of the most damaging to strike in this section."

Spencer wrote in the September 28, 1944, edition of The Hyde County Herald that Hyde is often knocked down but never out by storms and rain, pointing out that when crops are cut short by acts of Nature, citizens turn to sound and creeks for a livelihood, and that good hunting provides jobs for many in season.

1954 HURRICANE HAZEL

In October, 1954, Hurricane Hazel roared across the Outer Banks, across Pamlico Sound and up Pamlico River, causing abnormally high tides which inundated the area, and high winds which blew down trees and power lines, disrupting the area for a couple of days before order could be restored. We lived on East Main street in Washington at the time and the basement of the property we rented filled when the tide backed around from Jack's Creek, crossed Old Second street and came up behind our house. Mr. Joe Rickards was City Manager and rented the other side of the house. He got Pop Bowen and some volunteer firemen to drive one of the pumper trucks around back of the house and pump the tide water from the basement.

A year after Hazel, Hurricane Barbara visited the Outer Banks and did considerable damage. Then followed in succession Connie, Dianne and Ione. Editor and Publisher Ashley Futrell wrote in "The Washington Daily News" the day after Ione, "All I own is owned by Ione."

Coordination of efforts between emergency organizations such as County Emergency Preparedness, Salvation Army and

Red Cross, plus better communications, all combine to prepare the public for hurricanes, tornadoes and other natural disasters.

CHAPTER TWO

SHIP WRECKS

THE SCHOONER "COX"

The schooner "Cox" sank during a fierce storm off the coast of Hatteras October 2, 1880. Nana's mother, Jane, was first married to Litchfield Styron, who was one of the crew of this ill-fated ship. Others were Richard (Dick) Burrus, master, who was brother of Jane Burrus Styron; Litchfield Styron, who was father of Nana's half-sister, Janie; William Allen Ballance, Russell Austin, George L. Styron and Walter Gaskill. All perished when the "Cox" sank. Aunt Janie was born after her father drowned at sea so she really never knew him. Later, her mother married Henry Bunyan Stowe, and Nana was the first of eight children born to this union. It was always said that she was named "Janette" instead of "Jeanette" because of being born next after Aunt Janie. At any rate, she used "Janette" and other members of the family spelled it both ways. She was always affectionately known as "Cousin" Janette, "Miss" Janette, or "Aunt" Janette.

THE "CARROLL A. DEERING"

Grandpop recalled the wreck of the "Carroll A. Deering," a five-master which ran aground at Diamond Shoals January 31, 1921, a couple of years before I was born. He recollected that he was one of the first to get to her after the seas had calmed. He said she was breaking up and that all sails were still set. It was always said around Hatteras that the only sign of life aboard was a gray Maltese cat which was the father of several generations of gray cats found at various locations in the village. What happened to the ill-fated crew of the "Carroll A. Deering" remains today one of the well-kept secrets of the "Graveyard of the Atlantic." It is one of the classics of Outer Banks mysteries that has been written about in numerous articles and books, most notable of which is David Stick's publication entitled, "Graveyard of the Atlantic," a book about the hundreds of shipwrecks up and down the Outer Banks.

CANNABILISM

Another story Grandpop liked to tell was of the schooner which went aground near Hatteras and one of two known instances of cannibalism that actually took place on the Outer Banks. Robert L. Terrell wrote of this incident in a front-page article carried in the Thursday, July 25, 1957 edition of "The Belhaven Pilot". Terrell wrote that "the recent re-appearance of the remains of the big five-masted schooner CARROLL DEERING, Ghost Ship of Diamond Shoals, at a point near Hatteras Inlet, recalls the singular loss of the coasting schooner PATTIE MARTIN, which vessel was wrecked some 90 years ago this January not far distant from the site where wreckage of the DEERING was washed ashore following Hurricane Ione.

"Never in the 109-year old history of this Inlet has there been a more tragic, more heart-rending tale of human suffering than that which befell the unfortunate crew of the 57-ton register coasting schooner PATTIE MARTIN of Elizabeth City, N. C. Her loss off the bar at the entrance to Hatteras Inlet during the gale of January 7, 1866 records one of the two known instances in which cannibalism is actually known to have taken place here on the Outer Banks. Oddly enough one George Tolson, a resident of this island, was one of the participants in the affair," **wrote Mr.**

Terrell. He continues, "The PATTIE MARTIN, under command of Captain Dennis M. Smith of Camden, New Jersey, was blown off her regular course by a heavy northerly gale which set in upon her during the morning of January 6. Shortly before midnight of the following day the schooner was carried onto the outermost bar of the inlet, several miles offshore. Almost immediately she came apart at her seams, filling with water. Angry seas swept the vessel from stem to stern, sending her deck load of lumber into the ocean.

"Without other alternative her captain and crew took refuge in the ship's rigging where they lashed themselves to the foremast, momentarily safe from the fury of the storm. Their deliverance was short-lived, however, for within three hours from the time she had grounded her captain perished -- frozen to death by the biting cold of winter. Half an hour afterwards the cook, a Negro man, also perished from exposure. Two men -- George Tolson of Hatteras Island, and Harrison J. Steelman, the mate -- remained lashed to the wreck. For four days they remained on board the doomed vessel, momentarily expecting to see their ship go to pieces beneath them and themselves to share the fate of their companions. On the fourth day the seas moderated somewhat, and the two survivors were able to cut the body of the dead cook free from the rigging. On his frozen remains they subsisted another 48 hours until at last a pilot-boat from Ocracoke came to their relief and brought them safely ashore. Both Tolson and Steelman were in a most deplorable condition -- at the point of complete exhaustion -- their arms and legs badly frost-bitten. Neither, however, offered complaint about their subsistence on human flesh when questioned by a reporter who had been assigned to cover the disaster for a Northern newspaper."

CAPE HATTERAS LIGHTHOUSE

I recollect that in 1936 the mighty Atlantic Ocean was encroaching on the base of Cape Hatteras Lighthouse. The U. S. Coast Guard decided in 1936 to abandon the lighthouse and transferred ownership to the National Park Service. A skeleton lighthouse was built in the dunes on the back road in Buxton, to take place of the abandoned structure. This was used until 1950 when the old lighthouse was reactivated by the Coast Guard under a special use permit from the National Park Service.

Meantime, a radar dome was constructed atop the skeleton structure and this became the site of the Cape Hatteras Weather Bureau where important radar and weather information was generated and beamed around the world.

In order to keep the beach built up around the recommissioned Cape Hatteras Lighthouse, sand was pumped from Pamlico Sound onto the beach, but soon eroded away because of sand from the sound being of much finer texture than ocean sand. Large sandbags were then used to help reinforce the beach, along with concrete groins and the planting of sea oats, but all measures could not stop the encroaching Atlantic.

Along about this time people began to debate whether to abandon the old lighthouse again and leave it for the ocean to claim, or to move it to another location further inland. Several groups, both for and against relocation, were formed, and powerful arguments were presented by all sides to either leave it alone, or move it.

In 1998 a Request for Proposals to relocate the lighthouse was issued and a contract was awarded to International Chimney Corporation of Buffalo, N. Y., to move the historic structure to a new location. Funding for the project was supported in the House of Representatives by Congressman Walter Jones, Jr., and in the Senate by Sen. Lauch Faircloth. A total of $9.8 million was appropriated, and National Park Service agreed with International Chimney to proceed with the project, but the Dare County Board of Commissioners, who had been against the project, filed a motion for a Temporary Restraining Order to halt or delay the proceedings.

In 1999 the Dare County lawsuit was dismissed as well as another, and final plans were made to start the move in June, 1999. Moving progress was much better than first predicted, and aided by hydraulic pushers, the historic structure started its journey

June 17, 1999, at 3:05 PM, when it was nudged four inches to the southwest and began its 2,900 foot journey to its new location.

Large crowds of tourists and natives gathered each day to view the proceedings. Thousands of feet of video, and thousands of still photographs, have been taken. Media coverage beamed out every inch of progress to an anxious and eager world. Some had said the old structure would not stand being moved and would cave in. But the engineers for the project knew better, and finally on July 9, 1999, the lighthouse was pushed the final 79 feet to its new resting place.

Originally, the move was expected to take from four to six weeks, but because of new techniques employed by the engineers in charge of the project, it was accomplished in 23 days, including two days when no movement was made.

In the National Park Service's daily reports of the move, the question was frequently asked, "Have we done the right things?" Some people viewed the project as destroying history. Others said it was something that had to be done to preserve the history of the structure. The Park Service took the position of letting visitors to the site 100 years from now supply answers to the questions. Park Service's position is that "what we have done has been for them and for the preservation of our nation's great maritime heritage."

On July 17, 1999, at 4:00 PM, the Cape Hatteras Lighthouse was lowered to its permanent elevation, supported by cribbing towers below the main beams.

Meantime, what happened to the skeleton structure in Buxton woods? It was replaced with new radar facilities at Norfolk, VA, Wilmington, NC, and Newport, NC, along with weather satellites. The new Doppler Radar System is an improvement over conventional radar because it sees the velocity of motion in a storm and can approximate the amount of rain to be received and can measure echo tops of storms. The overlapping of the Doppler radar and weather satellites allows for continuous tracking of storms. The Weather Service shares the use of the Doppler with the Defense Department and the Federal Aviation Agency. The private sector can contract with National Weather Service. Radio and television stations along with private forecasters use these services.

CHAPTER THREE

INTERESTING DOCUMENTS

In the Beaufort County Register of Deeds office there are some interesting documents pertaining to shipping and storms in the early 1700's. In Book 3, Page 24, the following appears and is copied verbatim:

NORTH CAROLINA
BEAUFORT COUNTY

By this public instrument of protest, be it made known and manifest unto all whom these presents shall come, or whom it doth or may concern, that on the 30th of October anno 1749 and 23rd year of the reign of the King George of Great Brittain and before me John Riensett, one of his Majesties Justices of the Peace in and for the County of Beaufort in North Carolina and residing at Bath Town -- personally came and appeared William Downs Cherry, master, Philip Galaway, carpenter, and George Way, mariner lately belonging to the ship Dolphin who being severally sworn on the Holy Evangelists of Almighty God, made oath and declared as follows, viz: that on the 29th June last past they sailed from Boston New England in the ship Dolphin bound for Ocracoke Inlet in the port of Bath in North Carolina and from thence to London, that on the 3rd day of August following they arrived at Ocracoke and moored and unrigged in Beacon Island harbour, that on 7th day of October following, then lying moored and unrigged in Beacon Island harbour afs'd there arose a most violent storm of wind and rain from the N. E. by which the sloop called the Endeavour of Boston, Isaac Chitendon, master, lying in said harbour drove on the Ship Dolphin's bow and occasioned said ship to part two cables she had out to the eastward and obliged her to ride by one cable and anchor; that on the 8th day of October at 4 o'clock in the morning the ships other anchor started and the said ship was drove on the shoals where she lay beating till nine o'clock, that the wind then shifting to the S. W. drove said ship off the shoal, when the wind being extremely violent and seas boisterous, the Master and crew cut away the said ship's masts in order she might ride, and prevent her driving out of the harbour or on the shoal, nevertheless, the violence of the wind and seas kept said ship from driving her anchor not holding; which obliged master and crew to cut away the cable to prevent the ship's driving on the north breakers of Ocracoke Barr, a dangerous shoal, notwithstanding all their endeavors, the said ship was drove on the North breakers of Ocracoke Barr, where she beat her rudder off and part of her sheathing, that the sea being very high and boisterous pooped them several times and stove in their deadlights, that the said ship making a great deal of water, obliged them to keep both pumps going, and in this condition were drove to sea, where they continued till about one o'clock afs'd 8th of October, when said ship Dolphin was drove by the violence of the wind and seas on shore on Ocracoke Island, where said ship had not long struck, until the seas hove her broad side to the shore and made a free passage over her, so that the crew could not stand to the pumps, and soon occasioned 5 foot water in the hold, and the storm still continuing, the seas hove the said ship on her broad side. The said deponents declare, that, on a survey made by several masters and a carpenter of ship Dolphin, then lying on shore on Ocracoke Island, they found her stranded and settled much in the sand, her rudder off, her stern part broken in to and her planks started and her back broke, so that said ship could not be got and rendered unfit for service, for all which reasons afs'd William

Downes Cherry, Philip Galaway and George Way carpenter belonging to ship Dolphin, and I afs'd Justice at their request do solemnly protest against afs'd storms winds and seas for all damages suffered and to be suffered in and to said ship Dolphin and occasioned by the causes afs'd, this done at Bath day and year afs'd.

John Riensset, hand and seal

Wm Downes Cherry, Philip Galaway & George Way

This account is recorded in Book 3 at Page 25, also copied verbatim:

NORTH CAROLINA
BEAUFORT COUNTY

By this public act or instrument of protest be it made known and manifest unto all whom it may concern; that on the day of the date hereof before me Robert Boyd Esq one of his Majesties Justices of the Peace in the county of Beaufort in the province afs'd personally came and appeared Samuel Wakely mate, Jonathan Hodgkins and David Tory, mariners belonging to the Sloop Sarah, and made oath on the Holy Evangelists, that on the twenty fourth day of May last, about nine of the clock in the morning, being at an anchor in Lyn-haven bay, the said Sloop was taken by a Spanish Privateer schooner, the commander whereof put eight Spaniards and a Linguistor on board of the said sloop, in order to have carried the said vessel to the Havanna or St. Augustine; and the said Spaniards being unskillful navigators, were obliged to entrust these deponents with the care and management of the said sloop who kept hovering about the coast between Cape Hatteras and Cape Henry till the fifteenth of June following, at which time the parting of the mast giving way they prevailed on the said Spaniards to suffer them to cut away the mast to go ashore in the boat to get a spar, and that David Tory, together with two Spaniards and the Linguistor went on shore, where he met with Ezekial Farrow and acquainted him with these deponents condition, when the said Ezekial Farrow with two other men promised that night they would go off to the sloop to assist them; but the weather would not then permit; next day these deponents cut away the mast and then desired leave to go ashore to grind their axes, the said David Tory with two Spaniards and the Linguistor went on shore, where they met with the s'd Ezekial Farrow, Richard Barber and George Scarborough, Jacob Farrow, Francis Dawson, William Scarborough, James W., Joshua Wall and Francis P., all inhabitants of North Carolina, assembled together under a _____ assisted and helped these deponents to secure the s'd Spaniards and the Linguistor: and then went on board the said sloop, retook her and secured all the Spaniards and sent them to Edenton, and then deponents were obliged to unload part of the loading, to wit 427 bushels of wheat, 200 bushels of corn, 21 barrels of pork, one barrel of hogs fat and about 5 1/2 tons of iron to raise a new mast, the wind serving Northerly, these deponents proceeded to Ocracoke and came into the said port on the day of the date hereof; and the afs'd mate and mariners do further testify and declare that they used their utmost endeavors to prevent the aforesaid losses and damages for the benefit of the owners of the afs'd sloop. Wherefore the said mate and mariners have desired to make publication, that being taken by the Privateer afs'd at the time and place afs'd was the occasion of the damage done to the said vessel and cargo on board the sloop; therefore they do publicly and solemnly protest against all damages that hath or happens by reason of the s'd enemy's privateer.

In testimony whereof I have hereunto set my hand and seal this sixth day of July, in the twenty second year of the reign of our Sovereign Lord George the second, King of Great Brittain Rex anno dom 1748.

Another deposition appears in Book 3 at Page 25 as follows:

NORTH CAROLINA
BEAUFORT COUNTY

By this public instrument of protest be it made known and manifest unto whom these presents shall come, or whom it doth or may concern, that on the 10th day of January in the year 1749 and in the 23rd year of the reign of King George of Great Brittain, before me Robert Boyd Esq one of his Majesties Justices of the Peace, in and for the county of Beaufort in North Carolina and residing at Bath Town, personally came and appeared Joseph Wadley master and Samuel Holyoak belonging to the Brigantine Two Friends, who being severally sworn on the Holy Evangelists of Almighty God, made oath and declared as follows, viz: that on the 24th of November last past, they sailed from Boston in New England, and being in the latitude of 39 degrees and 40 minutes they met with a very hard gale of wind, and shipped very much water, the damage yet unknown; and these deponents do further testify and declare that the pumps were not neglected, wherefore the said master and mariners have desired to make this publication, that the wind and weather, which happened at the time and place afs'd, was the occasion of the damage done to the cargo on board, and therefore they do protest against the said wind and weather and all damages that happened to the cargo on board thereby; and I the afs'd Justice at their request do solemnly protest against the afs'd wind and weather and seas for all damages happened, or to be suffered to the cargo on board occasioned by the causes afs'd. Given under my hand and seal at Bath Town the day and year afs'd.

R. Boyd JP (SEAL)

Joseph Wadley
Samuel Holyoak

PART FIVE

CHAPTER ONE

SENSE OF HUMOR

Most Outer Bankers have a sense of humor and delight in telling stories about themselves or someone else. Men would gather around net scaffolds while mending chores were going on and see who could tell the biggest lie, and at other times in Mr. Damon Gray's barber shop. Women would gather in the afternoons on each others' porches to share the latest news, called by some as GOSSIP. Some of the humorous stories I have shared down through the years came from some of these gatherings, and Grandpop Irv always had a good story. One of his favorite yarns was about how Hatteras got its name. As related by him it went like this:

"In olden days when ships sailed up and down the coast a schooner ran aground just beyond the surf during a nor-easter. A beach vendue was being held the next morning. The wind was still fresh and blowing a near gale. A lady was standing atop a sand dune watching the proceedings, having to hold her skirts down with one hand and a wide-brimmed hat with the other. Women wore five or six petticoats and long dresses in those days. A hard flaw lifted the lady's skirts up around her knees. Whereupon she had to remove the hand that was holding her hat in order to hold down both sides of her skirts to keep her modesty. The hat blew into the sea, causing her to exclaim 'Well, young'uns, h'it was either hat'er'ass!'-- and that's how Hatteras got its name." Actually, the name originated with the tribe of Hatterask Indians that inhabited the Outer Banks long before the islands were settled by the White man.

BEST SHOT

Often times the men would sit around with a piece of juniper or cypress whittling and telling yarns. They would try to out-lie each other -- a sort of Outer Banks Liar's club. Grandpop was telling the group of the time he was a cook on a coastal schooner sailing between Philadelphia and the West Indies.

"We were abreast Georgetown, South Carolina, and the wind was blowing fresh from the sou'west. The captain decided we should put into port and wait for the wind to die down before continuing. While we were in port the captain asked me to take his old muzzle-loader ashore and fire it, since it hadn't been fired in a long time and needed a good cleaning out. I was walking along the beach looking for a good shot when I spotted three blackbirds perched on a telegraph wire. I didn't know whether to shoot the blackbirds or wait for a better shot. About that time I spied a rattlesnake just a few feet in front of me, coiled and ready to strike. I didn't know whether to shoot the three blackbirds or the rattlesnake. I looked over to my left and there was an eight-point buck standing in the rushes. I didn't know whether to shoot the three blackbirds, the rattlesnake, or the buck. All of a sudden I heard a rustling in the marsh to my right, and there sat 12 mallards. I didn't know whether to shoot the three blackbirds, the rattlesnake, the buck or the 12 mallards! I then remembered the advice my old pappy had always given me -- 'aim high, son, and shoot straight!' I took aim at the three blackbirds and pulled the trigger. The shot hit the blackbirds and killed them, the ramrod hit the rattlesnake and killed it, a piece of the barrel flew over and killed the buck, the remainder of the barrel scattered amongst those 12 mallards and killed them, and the recoil knocked me back into a sow with eight pigs and killed them. And that was the best shot I ever made!"

NEXT BEST SHOT

There's always a "next best shot". Grandpop said he was working as a cook on the government dredge in Philadelphia Harbor. In those days they didn't have the modern refrigeration methods of today, and all fresh meat had to come from hunting in the woods. Grandpop said he'd been out in the woods hunting all day and had used all his ammunition except for one ball and enough powder to fire it from his trusty muzzle loader. He hadn't bagged anything and was getting ready to leave when he spied a wild boar out of the corner of his eye. He was taking aim when out of the corner of his other eye he spotted a wildcat. Both were within range, but he had only one shot. Thinking fast, he jumped behind a log, pulled his knife from its sheath, stuck it in the log, and as the wildcat and boar came nearer he pointed the gunbarrel down the middle of the blade, pulled the trigger, the blade splitting the ball with half hitting the wildcat and killing it, and the other half hitting the boar and killing it. He said that was the second best shot he ever made!

ALL WET!

Nana and Grandpop were married in 1901. Nana loved to tell the story about Grandpop preparing to go set-netting early one morning when she decided she would go with him. She said Grandpop tried every way he knew to dissuade her but she insisted on going. The sail skiff was tied to a stake about 100 feet from the landing in knee-deep water. Grandpop was in the skiff and Nana, with her coattails in hand, finally worked her way across the side. She said Grandpop picked her up and threw her overboard, saying, "Now, what do you say about that?" Nana said that she replied, "I say you're a s. o. b." She said she waded ashore still cussin' Irv under her breath. Irv's father, Mr. Ira, was standing on the shoreside and said, "Janette, what has that rascal done to you?" And she replied, "Well, didn't you see him throw me overboard!" And Granpop Ira said "I'll settle with him when he gets back." Nana said, "You won't have the privilege 'cause I'm gonna kill him!" When Irv got back ashore and was walking up the path to the house, he came to the door and threw his hat in and said, "If the hat can stay in, can I come in?" Nana said she jumped at him and ran him around the yard. She said they had a lot of fun kidding each other. Those were happy days for the young married couple.

DIPPIN' AND CHEWIN'

The art of dippin' snuff and chewin' terbaccer may be a lost one in some sections of the country, but at least tobacco chewin' seems to still be in vogue in these parts. And if the truth were known a lot of women still "sneak" a dip now and then when nobody is around to detect! (In polite conversation it is called "having a social.") Nana would blend some Lorrilard salt with Society sweet and put it in her favorite "tin". She'd send us to the trash pile to retrieve empty cans (called tins) to hold the spittle when the ladies would congregate on the front porch to discuss the latest. Nana would get me to chew her "toothbrushes" which consisted of cutting a twig of sweetgum (or similar sweet-tasting wood) and chewing one end until it became spread enough to constitute a "brush" on which snuff was "dipped" as the ladies carried on a conversation. Some shunned the "toothbrush" and went directly to the lower lip by shaking out the desired portion, often beating the tin against the teeth to get the desired amount. Inevitably some would fall on their blouse and they'd dust it off with a handkerchief. If I was nearby I would always get some up my nose and start sneezing!

SOURCES OF NEWS

In addition to their own sources, these ladies always welcomed the arrival of a drummer, which was an occasion to catch up on tidbits of news from the villages up and down the Banks. Since Hatteras was one of the last on the route, the news by then was considerable. These traveling salesmen would ply their trade by calling door-to-door, selling everything from headache powders to furniture. Nana would purchase from the Watkins representative some good-smelling starch along with the usual patent medicines she used to doctor family members including liniment, rubbing alcohol, headache tablets, purgatives, red balsam, mercurochrome and iodine, and a box or two of assorted bandages and adhesives. Visits by these drummers afforded contact with the outer world. It was not uncommon for them to pay visits of one or more hours, and if they arrived at mealtime they were always invited to stay. When the snuff-dipping sessions took place on the front porch, much of the news gleaned from contact with the drummers would be shared all over again!

"The Daily Advance" from Elizabeth City,"The Virginian Pilot" out of Norfolk, and "The Dare County Times", a weekly published by Victor Meekins in Manteo, were other sources of news to those who could afford the subscription. We young'uns were sent up the road to the Post Office to get the mail. We'd step up to the window, peer through the bars, and ask, "Any mail for Miss Janette?" We delighted in getting the various mail order catalogues, which, when thoroughly perused and dog-eared, would then be placed in the two-seater toilet out back to be used for you-know-what. "The Dare County Times" later was changed to "The Coastland Times." Mr. Meekins was a protege of W. O. Saunders, the crusty editor and publisher of" The Elizabeth City Independence", known for his personal style of journalism where every article carried his own editorial opinion. Saunders and Meekins would, as we would say these days, "call a spade a spade", or "tell it like it is!" I distinctly remember a headline "The Coastland Times" carried one day declaring "County Funds Being Pistaway". Mr. Meekins wrote a weekly column and later compiled these into a book entitled, "The Old Sea Captain and the Drummer". He was another of those "institutions" of the Outer Banks.

PLENTY OF GAS

Geneva Braddy of Bath and I were married in 1950. By then the State Highway Department had started construction of the road from Oregon Inlet to Hatteras. One crew was working from the north (Oregon Inlet to Rodanthe) and another from Hatteras to Avon. Uncle Harvey said the worst thing that ever happened to the Outer Banks was when "they built that d----- road and turned all them touristers in here!" You could get a rebuttal on that argument from others who depend on the tourist trade to bring in much-needed revenue to boost the economy. In 1951 Geneva and I took the bus to Engelhard and boarded the "Hadeco" for the trip across the sound to Hatteras. Milton

Meekins was cap'n and Mr. Isaiah Ballance was mate. Milton grew up next door to my grandparents and Nana considered him "one of her boys" since she attended his mother, Nancy Jane, when he came into the world. When the "Hadeco" docked at Hatteras Development Co. we were observing a tanker make her way through the harbor entrance with its deck awash, being loaded to the gunwhales with gasoline to be discharged in bulk tanks ashore. Geneva had watched the progress of this vessel and finally she asked, "What kind of ship is that?" I explained that it was a tanker bringing gasoline from Norfolk to be stored ashore. She mused for a moment, then said: "Well, there's one thing for sure. She won't have to worry about running out of gas!"

WHAT'S IN A NAME?

I worked as Sports Editor of "The Washington Daily News" from June, 1951 until December of 1964 when I went into the Register of Deeds office. When Editor and Publisher Ashley Futrell was running for the State Senate in 1960 he asked me to contact some of my kinfolks on the Outer Banks to help in his campaign. I started in Manteo and worked my way down to Avon and Buxton before getting to Hatteras and talking with many people whom I had known over the years. Later, Ashley made a follow-up trip down the Banks himself. He delights in telling the following story:

"I was visiting in the Blue Marlin Marina and talking with Edison Meekins, and in the course of our conversation I told him that I had a young fellow working for me who had family connections in Hatteras, and he asked me who it was? I told him his name was John Morgan. Edison shook his head and said as how he didn't really know anyone by that name. I told him, 'Well, you ought to know him. He said he spent all his summers here when he was a little boy.' Edison scratched his head, looked at me and asked, 'Who did he stay with when he was here?' When I told him that his grandmother's name was Janette Stowe, Edison exclaimed, 'My Lord, why didn't you say so. You mean <u>JOHN IRVIN</u>!'" Mr. Futrell said that he found that when inquiring about me around Hatteras if he used the first two names of John Irvin he could get a response, but if he asked if anyone knew of John Morgan, nobody had ever heard of me! Many of the natives figured my last name was Stowe, since I stayed with my Stowe grandparents and had all Stowe relatives in the area.

CHAPTER TWO

MAKING YOUR OWN AMUSEMENT

In the 1930's children had to make their own amusement and many homemade articles were born of necessity. We would make little cars out of match boxes and cotton spools and play underneath the house, making tracks around the brick pillars, out into the yard, and back underneath. We'd save our sucker sticks and use them to build little log cabins and garages for the matchbox cars. The sticks from popsicles also were used for making items of handicraft. Another favorite was to get the ring from the staff end of a net, fashion a loop in the end of a stiff piece of wire, and push the ring (or hoop) along with the wire. If one wanted something larger he could use a barrel stave, or a worn-out automobile tire pushed along with a stick of wood. Homemade scooters were made from surplus pieces of board and discarded roller skates or wagon wheels.

Mr. Rube Stowe purchased for his boys, Dallas and Walter, a set of boxing gloves and everyone in the neighborhood took a turn boxing each other. If I have cauliflower ears today it is because Walter Stowe pounded away on both sides of my head every time we put on the gloves. I could never parry his vicious hooks coming from both sides! Occasionally there would be a bloody nose or black eye, but most of the time we broke up on a friendly basis. If one or the other got hit and flew mad, one of the older boys would break us up until we had time to cool off. We played a game called "me-honky" which was something like hide and go-seek. We had all kinds of good hiding places around the church yard, in the church, around the houses in the neighborhood, up trees, in the marsh, and in the graveyard in front of Nana's house. Aunt Mable used to say, "Go out there to the corner of the graveyard and ask Uncle so-and-so what he's doing there, and he'll say 'nothing'". She fooled us on this several times before we caught on to the fact that someone buried in the graveyard actually says nothing!

BANKER PONIES

Before the government took them off the island in the mid 1930's, wild ponies roamed the dunes and woods of the Outer Banks, and many a young boy had his own pony which he had broken and claimed for his own. It was told by old-timers that these ponies came from Arabian stock off ships that wrecked along the coast in the late 1700's and early 1800's. Those who could afford them had saddles and all the trimmings, and those who could not made do with a simple bridle and bit and rode bareback. One fellow controlled his pony by pulling to either side on the mane. Often times a race would be arranged on the beach and wagers would be taken on who the winners would be in each race. Some folks had homemade carts pulled by these ponies. Later it was determined that the stock was depleting the natural foliage which is so essential to holding the sandy land together, that the ponies had to be done away with, so a big roundup was held, the ponies were penned, and shipped off the island to places like Chincoteague, Va., and other habitats for this variety of horse. On Ocracoke Island the ponies were allowed to remain, but had to be penned. Today one can see these enclosures as you drive down NC Highway 12 into Ocracoke Village. Pony penning events are still held at Ocracoke.

FAMILY SONG FESTS

Other than the movies and an occasional Saturday night outing at the beach dance spots, one had to seek and make his own entertainment. Uncle Harvey had a guitar he had ordered from Sears and Roebuck, I had a jews harp I had gotten in a box of popcorn, while others used waxed paper covering a comb to hum a tune, sort of like a "bazooka" which was a tin instrument with a piece of waxed paper in a circled enclosure near the mouthpiece. The purpose of the waxed paper was to vibrate the voice as it went through the instrument. It was all homemade, but it suited the musical tastes of those in the household. Grandpop had bought Nana a peddle-type organ with the stops over the keyboard. It was always a delight when family members would gather around, Nana would seat herself on the bench, and having been self-taught and playing by ear, she'd strike up some of the old familiar hymns we all loved to sing. One could hear us all the way up to the middle of the village singing "The Old Rugged Cross", "Crossing the Bar", "Just As I Am", "Kneel At The Cross", "In The Sweet Bye and Bye", and several more.

GOIN' TO CHURCH

The Methodist Church was located across the road from my grandparents' home. On sunny summer Sunday mornings one could hear Miss Nancy Jane Meekins and other members of the choir half way through the village as their voices carried long and far through the open windows of the church. Prior to union in 1939 there were two Methodist churches at Hatteras. The North'ard Methodist Church was located "down the road" and this was the one my grandparents attended. The South'ard Methodist Church was located "up the road" and was the one established after the War Between the States. It took a long time to get over the wounds and scars of differences generated following the Civil War, but finally in 1939 the Methodists decided to get back together, and following this union the north'ard church closed and was later sold. The "up the road" church remains today as the main congregation on the island, with the Assembly of God, a Pentecostal church, being the other.

Mr. Deck Oden was our Sunday School teacher. He was a kindly, gentle man who had a way with growing boys. Our class consisted of two benches in the northwest corner of the building. Other classes occupied other pews around the room. Teachers had to talk in low tones so as not to disturb the other groups. After Sunday School we would go outside and see who could jump the fence around the churchyard, winding up most of the time on our rearends with grass stains on our clean, white duck trousers which had just arrived in the mail from Sears & Roebuck and purchased with our hard-earned crab and clam money.

Preacher Winslow from Hertford came down one summer to hold a revival. He played the trombone (it could be heard all over the island) and sang lustily -- in the great Methodist tradition. He could get sinners to come to the rail and repent -- but the next day many repenters would become what is known in Methodist circles as "BACKSLIDERS!" Nana invited the preacher to "come spend all day" as was the custom in those times. I got wind of this and disappeared under the house where I spent the day! Nana came out on the porch several times and hollered for me, as was her custom, but I kept my silence in my secret hiding place under the house until the preacher left!

Dr. Maynard O. Fletcher, who was president of Washington Collegiate Institute, a church-sponsored "finishing school" located in Washington Park, had a summer home up the road a short distance from the church. It was located next to the parsonage. E. Frank Ruble came out of the Holston Conference of East Tennessee and was a teacher at W. C. I., later becoming principal at Washington High School. I remember seeing him grimace whenever "Northern Methodist Church" would be mentioned in his presence. He avowed there was no such thing -- that it was then known as "The Methodist Episcopal Church" and the other congregation was known as "The Methodist Episcopal Church - South."

My mother, Katherine, finished her schooling at Hatteras, consisting of eight grades, and as was the custom of those on the Outer Banks at the time, came to Washington to "finishing school" to complete her education. She was taught by Mr. Ruble and Dr. Fletcher. Others from Outer Banks communities would go to Elizabeth City and New Bern to "finishing schools." My mother got a job in Mr. John Willis' bakery, met my father who was a clerk working in Mr. Harry McMullan, Sr.'s law office, and they married in 1921. On July 11, 1923, their first son, John Irvin, was brought into the world by Dr. E. M. Brown. My brother, Richard Bailey Morgan, was born January 18, 1925, died Tuesday, June 14, 1994, age 69.

FUN IN A SAILSKIFF

Mr. Rube Stowe had a sprit-sail skiff he used for set netting and going to his pound nets. His youngest son was Walter and whenever Mr. Rube was home from fishing trips in the sound, he would let us use the sail skiff. She was the sailingest sail skiff

I've ever seen. Sails were made of canvas before the lighter synthetic materials were invented. A sprit would be placed in a rope loop at the upper right-hand corner of the sail, with the base being placed in another loop in a rope tied around the lower mast that could be inched up or down to either tauten or loosen the sail. A boom was used when on a beat to get full use of the mainsail when heading into the wind. Walter was my age and we enjoyed many hours of pleasant cruising around Oliver's Reef and beyond, sailing in and out of thunder squalls, tying up to the Oliver's Reef lighthouse and fishing for sheepshead using mud fiddlers for bait, taking a swim and having a great time in general. Sailors refer to sailing with the wind as a run. We called it "fair to the wind." A reach was "side-to-the-wind" and a beat was called "headin' into the wind." When a boat is underway it pulls a wake behind it. We called this "draggin' a sea." You could get your noggin knocked off if you failed to duck the boom on a tack. When sailing fair with the wind, we would push the jib out to port with an oar (this was called "goosewinging") while the main was on the starboard. We'd get on the crest of a wave and virtually fly! This we called "gettin' her out on a fly!" The skiff would plane, skimming over the surface like a surf board.

     Occasionally Mr. Rube would let us sail out to the channel with him to fish the nets. We'd sort the fish and have them ready to go into boxes, ice them down, and get the sales tickets and be back home in time for breakfast which consisted for the most part of bread and coffee. I can hear my grandmother now, when someone would walk by her kitchen door of a morning and inquire, "What're ye' havin' fer breakfast, Janette?" and she'd answer, "Bread and coffee. Come on in and have some!"

HOMEMADE SAILBOAT

Prior to leaving for Hatteras one summer, I had saved my pennies and bought a $1.25 sail boat from Woolworth's Department Store in Washington. I thought that sailboat was the prettiest thing I'd ever seen, and was sure it would far surpass anything the boys down at Hatteras would have. How wrong I was. The next day after our arrival we went to the landing to have our "maiden voyage" with this sleek sailing yacht, and all the kids were on hand to see what this store-bought marvel would do when put to the test. There's always a fresh sou-west breeze blowing from down Hatteras Inlet way during the summer months. I set the rudder, placed her in the water, and over she flopped on her side! Laughter greeted me from those assembled. "Hey, Washington, why don't you shorten up on the sheets?" Or, "You ought to add some more lead to the keel to keep her from flopping over," or, "you ought to have better sense than to try to sail a store-bought boat in these waters. That thing is made for a bath tub!" They didn't know what a bath tub was. All of them washed out of a wash pan and took a bath all over in a zinc wash tub, the same as I did!

I was crestfallen, to say the least. I went home crying, lugging that store-bought sail boat by its mast. Grandpop was home between trips to Elizabeth City. He heard me crying and asked what was wrong? I told him of my plight. "I'll make you a sailboat that they won't laugh at," he said. And he did. He went to his workshop and found an old goose decoy that had been damaged, cut off the top, and using the bottom half for the hull, he used a woodcutting tool to hollow it out, whittled out a mast, boom and sprit, got an old sheet and made a sail (Nana sewed the seams for us), put a center board and rudder on, and finally had her rigged for her maiden voyage. He advised me to get a couple of Bull Durham sacks and fill them with sand for ballast, just in case the wind freshened. We then headed for the landing. I knew enough from having observed Grandpop during construction of that sailboat that the center board and rudder had to be set at just the right angle in order for her to keep from luffing off and turning over. "Head her up into the wind," advised Grandpop, "and she'll hold her course." Well, that goose-belly sailboat out-sailed and out-maneuvered everything at the landing and I became the envy of all the other guys who then wanted to sail my boat while they tried to make improvements to their own.

SUMMER BASEBALL GAMES

Saturday afternoons during the summer were reserved for baseball games. Fierce competition existed between the villages of Hatteras, Ocracoke, Frisco (called Trent), Buxton (called Cape), and Avon (called Kinnakeet). Maurice Burrus had a short stint as a pitcher with Connie Mack's Philadelphia Athletics before developing a sore arm and returning to Hatteras where he was called on to pitch many games for the home team. Edgar Styron was also a strong-armed pitcher who'd throw his left leg high in the air and come down hard with his delivery. The ball diamond was located on the beach side of the road between The Beacon and Mr. Ellsworth Ballance's beach pavilion. Inevitably some of the older men would overindulge themselves with East Lake corn whisky and occasionally a free-for-all would break out, with players and fans alike engaging in the fray. Most of the time the umpire was a deaf-mute and there was no arguing with him!

A SUMMER SUNDAY'S OUTING

Myron (Clam) Stowe and Maynard (Speed) Stowe were the sons of Nelson Stowe, a cousin of my Grandpop Irv. Clam and Speed, along with Uncle Berry and others who had just returned from overseas duty in 1945, decided it would be a good idea to invite some of the pretty girls in the village for a Sunday boat ride on Mr. Nelson's "Ursula", named for his wife. Clam had been in the Army and was shot up pretty bad. He had a game leg which was braced causing him to use a cane to assist in his walking. The trip was arranged. All the gals were to pack a picnic basket, the boys were to bring the drinks to wash it down, and Clam and Speed were to furnish the transportation. Sunday dawned bright and clear, a perfect day for going outside. We headed out Hatteras Inlet on the "Miss Ursula" toward Diamond Shoals. Some of the girls got seasick although the boat was rolling easily on a slight swell. They got rid of their breakfasts over the side and went below to rest.

We pulled along side the Diamond Shoals Lightship and asked the bos'un if we could come aboard. He viewed all those pretty gals in shorts and halters and allowed as how it would be his and the crews' good pleasure to have the women come aboard, and that he didn't give a dern whether the men came or not! He was kidding, of course. Some of the crew hadn't seen a woman for probably three weeks so one can imagine their eagerness to have them come aboard. The bos'un threw fenders over the side to keep the "Ursula" from scraping the side of the lightship, then threw over the Jacobs ladder and came halfway down, lending a hand to help the girls up the ladder and over the side. The men followed. Needless to say members of the crew were more than delighted to show the ladies around the ship while the men were on their own. Lightships that once stood guard at Diamond and Frying Pan Shoals have long since been replaced by Texas Towers and automated lights that can be controlled from shore. Today's modern electronics in communications have done away with the necessity of the Texas Towers. Lightships played an important role in warning mariners of the dangers of those treacherous waters.

Fishing Fun - Uncle Harvey, left, Nana, center, and Geneva hold string of fish while I snap photo following great day of fishing near Hatteras Inlet.

PART SIX

CHAPTER ONE

CHANGES TAKE PLACE

With the completion by the State of the paved highway in the early 1950's, more and more tourist traffic was being turned into the villages from Oregon Inlet to Hatteras, necessitating a demand for ferry service to Ocracoke Island. The enterprising Frazier Peele secured a surplus landing craft, converted it to a ferry, and this was the forerunner of the present state-operated system in the area. The Midgette Brothers, Anderson, Stockton, and Harold, operated a bus service from Manteo to Hatteras. Later the Midgettes got into the real estate and motel business along with other natives who owned property and outside entrepreneurs who came in and purchased land for development. When the Herbert C. Bonner Bridge across Oregon Inlet was dedicated in May of 1964, more drastic changes came and a new way of life began to emerge for those living along the Outer Banks, with tourism taking a prominent role in the employment of people to build and staff the many motels and restaurants which sprang up. The Federal Government had established the Cape Hatteras National Seashore and this brought an influx of tourists from all over the nation. Trucks and large vans had already replaced freight boats as a means of bringing supplies in from the outside and of hauling fish to markets.

BEGAN AS CHALLENGE

Lindsay C. Warren devoted 45 years of his life to championing the cause of the Dare Coast area. It all began as a challenge.

Hon. Lindsay Carter Warren

People asked: "Why this so-called exceptional interest in Dare County?" and Mr. Warren's answer was this: "No other county in America can boast of the first English child being born on its soil."

He continued: No other county in the state can boast of the first airplane flight. Dare County has more coastline than almost all of the other counties along the N. C. Coast. Dare County abounds in history and famous shipwrecks. This was a great challenge, and I decided to do something about it."

Dare County possessed natural and historical advantages unlimited, and was trying to become a part of North Carolina with little apparent success at the time.

Mr. Warren was a candidate for the State Senate in 1916 and wanted to meet the people of Dare County. This is where his interest in the area was born.

During his early days in Congress, Mr. Warren recollected that his close friend, F. C. Kugler of Washington, N. C., was appointed by Governor Angus W. McLean to fill an unexpired term on the Highway Commission.

It was at this time that Mr. Warren prevailed on Mr. Kugler to go to the Dare Coast with him. "I pictured to him a road from Kitty Hawk eventually to Ocracoke, and his first reaction was that if he started such a project he would be run out of the state and called crazy," Mr. Warren said.

But by another year Mr. Kugler had become quite enthusiastic over the proposition, knowing that it would take years to accomplish but anxious to get started.

Mr. Kugler then built the highway on the beach from Kitty Hawk to the approaches into Manteo. At the same time a private corporation was building a bridge across Currituck Sound (a toll bridge, of course.)

Mr. Warren had several conferences with leading citizens and county authorities in Dare County about a bridge from the beach over to Roanoke Island, and the county built it as a toll bridge at the time. This was the beginning of several challenging and sometimes fiercely-fought battles for the Dare Coast area.

Ambassador Speaks

Mr. Warren invited Sir Esme Howard, the British Ambassador, to speak at Fort Raleigh on August 18, 1926, at the occasion of the celebration of the birth of Virginia Dare. Fort Raleigh was then nothing but a wilderness, but 5,000 folks came to Roanoke Island by boat for this great occasion, which marked the first grand scale observation of Virginia Dare's birth.

After this, in 1927, Mr. Warren introduced a bill in Congress to create a memorial to the Wright Brothers, to be located on Kill Devil Hill. At the time of the laying of the cornerstone for the Wright Memorial the Kugler road had not been completed; there was not a blade of grass on the beach nor any of the sand dunes; there were very few cottages in the old Nags Head section; and there were only three dilapidated old Coast Guard stations under which men, boats and horses had to abide.

Mr. Warren then initiated a program of getting up-to-date Coast Guard stations from the Virginia state line to Ocracoke. He was endeared to the hearts of several generations of Coast Guardsmen who had a rich heritage along the Outer Banks.

Meantime, work was continuing on the Wright Memorial. Kill Devil Hill was anchored (stabilized by the planting of grass), and with the completion of the new road the area began to develop and grow by leaps and bounds.

In 1937 Mr. Warren introduced in Congress a bill creating the Cape Hatteras National Seashore. The Congressman was one of three men living at that time who founded the Lost Colony. (Paul Green, who wrote the symphonic drama, and R. Bruce Etheridge, veteran Dare County legislator, were the other two).

Mr. Warren prevailed upon President Franklin D. Roosevelt to come down to Roanoke Island and view the Lost Colony pageant. A special train with the President and his party stopped at Elizabeth City, and they made the remainder of the journey by boat.

President Roosevelt asked Mr. Warren to announce to the very large crowd of 7,500 people that he (Roosevelt) had signed the Warren Bill for the creation of the Cape Hatteras National Seashore that day on Dare County soil.

This, too, was a momentous occasion in the development of the Dare Coast area.

Appeared To Be Doomed

Although out of Congress in 1940 to become Comptroller General of the United States, and although the fate of the Cape Hatteras Seashore appeared to be doomed, Conrad Wirth, the brilliant director of the National Park Service and a close personal friend of Mr. Warren, informed Mr. Warren that he believed he could convince the Mellon Foundation to put up money to buy land if the State would provide matching funds.

Later, Governor Kerr Scott discussed this proposition at length with Mr. Warren, as well as with Congressman Herbert C. Bonner who had succeeded Mr. Warren in Congress. Mr. Scott became an enthusiastic supporter of the project.

The Seashore project was bitterly fought by some of Mr. Warren's close friends. But Mr. Warren did not waver one second, believing it would turn out to be the best thing that could possibly happen to Dare County -- and this has already been proven.

At about this time a great hue and cry arose in Dare County and a few other Eastern counties to build toll bridges across Croatan Sound, Alligator River, and Oregon Inlet as well as a toll road up the beach to Virginia Beach. Mr. Warren opposed every single proposition, bucking at times some of his warmest personal friends on the subject of tolls.

He said then that it would be a crime to bottle up Eastern North Carolina. Tolls already had been removed from the Chowan River Bridge, the Wright Memorial Bridge, and the bridge over the sound to Manteo. The great free bridge built by Governor J.

C. B. Eringhaus over Albemarle Sound had just been completed. Mr. Warren said the sole credit for the Albemarle Sound bridge went to Governor Eringhaus. At the time it was the longest bridge in the state.

Consults With Umstead

In 1953, while still Comptroller General, Mr. Warren went to Raleigh to see his close friend, Governor William B. Umstead, who at the time was a very sick man and in bed at the Governor's Mansion.

The net result of this visit was that the Governor would build the toll-free Croatan Sound bridge, which today bears his name, the "William B. Umstead Memorial" bridge. I covered the dedication of this bridge. Ceremonies were held at the top of the fixed span, with the Elizabeth City High School band playing for the occasion and notables from the state and national governments on hand.

Governor Umstead thanked Mr. Warren for the strong fight that he was making against any toll bridges or toll roads and said, "Lindsay, I'm one hundred per cent with you and no one will ever say that William Umstead ever built a toll road or bridge anywhere in North Carolina."

Governor Umstead said in a public meeting several months later at Manteo that except for Lindsay Warren the Croatan Sound Bridge would have been delayed for many years.

This led up to the Alligator and Oregon Inlet bridge projects. The mighty edifice across Alligator River was at the time the third great bridge in Eastern North Carolina and just a few feet shorter than the Umstead Memorial bridge. It culminated another link in the long and hard fight Lindsay Warren and others made for the area. Warren's foresight and devotion to the area and its people made him a living memorial in which he was held in high respect and esteem. It was fitting and proper that the new bridge across Alligator River should bear his name, not that he wanted it that way because he always took the position that no public work should be named for any living person, and he did what he could to stop naming of this bridge after him. But the committee of representatives from the Second Senatorial District overruled Mr. Warren's objections and named the bridge after him anyhow.

Formal Dedication Cape Hatteras National Seashore

Thursday, April 24, 1958, was truly a red letter day in the history of the North Carolina Outer Banks, when the Cape Hatteras National Seashore was formally dedicated in two ceremonies, one at Cape Hatteras Lighthouse and the other at Coquina Beach on Bodie Island. A number of people whose contributions made possible the park were recognized at these exercises. A bronze plaque was unveiled commemorating the initial gift of 2,700 acres of land at Cape Hatteras by the family of Henry Phipps. Attending the ceremonies with Conrad Wirth, Director of the National Park Service at the time and for whom one of the Oregon Inlet Ferries was named, were Governor Luther Hodges, Hon. Lindsay C. Warren who as Congressman introduced legislation authorizing the park, and other notables of the federal and state governments. Roger C. Ernst, assistant Secretary of the Interior, made the dedication. Other notables on hand were Paul Mellon of the family which donated $1 million to buy land for the park; Congressman Herbert C. Bonner and Admiral H. C. Moore, commandant of the Fifth Coast Guard District, and Raymond R. Guest, a representative of the Phipps family who unveiled the tablet at Cape Hatteras.

The establishment of a seashore park was first advocated in the early 1920's when W. O. Saunders, Elizabeth City newspaper publisher, came out with bold headlines and maps advocating making the entire coast of North Carolina a great state park. It was an idea bold in conception for its time and found but a few people with sufficient vision or interest to grasp its possibilities and its worth to the people. It also faced a tremendous barrier in lack of sufficient state funds to finance such an undertaking. When Lindsay C. Warren of Beaufort County and representing the First Congressional District, got to Congress in 1924 a powerful advocate was added to the cause, and by the early 1930's he had enlisted strong support in Congress. For nearly ten years thereafter, government aid went into the project, first into reclamation projects, or the restoration of beaches which had been damaged by erosion. This was during the days of the CCC camps and the Transients when sand fences were built on the beaches to catch drifting sands and hold them in place.

In 1941, during the administration of Governor Broughton, the State of North Carolina spent its first funds in an effort to acquire land for the park. A commission of patriotic North Carolinians gave their efforts to the cause. An early and staunch advocate who put in a lot of hard work in behalf of the park and who enlisted the interest of the Phipps family was Frank Stick, who pioneered since 1920 in developments of superior beach colonies on the Dare Coast. The seashore park met with opposition from the beginning, mostly from those who feared loss of profits from real estate. Those opponents sometimes by misrepresentation of the actual possibilities of the park, aroused anti sentiment among others, but most came to see that the Seashore Park actually hurt nobody but was a great boon to the entire Outer Banks, making possible the development of many profitable business enterprises catering to a great number of tourists from across the nation attracted to the area through advertising and promotion in the various media. Like the proverbial pebble dropped in the pool, the establishment of the Seashore Park, the building of bridges to connect the area, and the other attractions already existing, all combined to bring a ripple effect which was a tremendous shot in the arm for a wavering economy that no longer could depend entirely on the fishing industry for a livelihood.

Oregon Inlet Bridge

The Southern Albemarle Association, composed of several coastal counties which came together in the 1950's for the purpose of advocating for bridges to bring the region closer together, had for years pushed for a bridge across Oregon Inlet after successfully campaigning for bridges across Albemarle Sound, Croatan Sound (named for Gov. William B. Umstead) and Alligator River (named for the late Congressman and Comptroller General Lindsay C. Warren). Up until this time the only access to the Outer Banks other than ferry service was the bridge from Point Harbor to Kitty Hawk. The Oregon Inlet bridge was completed in 1963 and dedicated on Saturday, May 2, 1964 in honor of the late Congressman Herbert C. Bonner who served the First Congressional District until his death in 1966. I covered the event for The Washington Daily News. It was a cool and windy day but did not thwart the gala festivities in connection with the program for the $4 million structure which connects lower Nags Head and Hatteras Island. The Congressman was introduced by Secretary of Commerce Luther H. Hodges who was Governor at the time the bridge project began. Also on hand was Governor Terry Sanford during whose term the bridge was built, along with a host of other dignitaries representing the State and Federal Highway Commissions and officials of the National Park Service. The curving structure has a gradual rise up to 62 feet above the Oregon Inlet channel where one can get a great view of the Atlantic Ocean on one side and Pamlico Sound on the other, with Bodie Island Lighthouse also being in view. It was completed and opened to traffic in November of 1963 but the dedication was delayed until the beginning of the tourist season in 1964.

Rep. Herbert C. Bonner, First Congressional District (right), and John Morgan, reporter for The Washington (N.C.) Daily News, at the dedication of the Herbert C. Bonner Bridge over Oregon Inlet, Saturday, May 2, 1964.

I also covered the dedication of the Lindsay C. Warren Bridge spanning Alligator River at East Lake. The ceremonies were held in Columbia, and on hand were dignitaries from the local, state and federal levels of government. Warren said, "The completion of this magnificent three-mile bridge comes as a fulfillment of a dream that it seemed would never come true. For many years disappointments and heartaches piled up. Many who had advocated it passed on. The Coastland Times for years wrote powerful and effective editorials for free bridges. It never wavered! The Southern Albemarle Association with tenacity and determination refused to give up and I know how happy that organization is today for they kept the torch burning. When anyone talks to me about the bridges, I always reply 'There is glory enough for all.'"

Mr. Warren, a staunch advocate and fighter for free bridges and a strong foe of tolls, continued by saying, "When the General Assembly of 1959 convened, the seven representatives and two senators from the Second Senatorial District immediately discussed the bridging of Alligator River and Oregon Inlet. I like to again publicly call out these names -- R. Bruce Etheridge of Dare, Charles Cohoon of Tyrrell, Frank Everett of Martin, Dr. J. M. Phelps, now deceased, of Washington, Dick O'Neal of Hyde, Ned Delamar of Pamlico, Wayland Sermons of Beaufort, Senator Elbert Peel, Jr., of Martin and myself. The group was kind enough to select me as its spokesman, although each one of them strongly and ably presented his views. We had abundant evidence to see how badly past efforts for the bridges had been bungled and mishandled. We found the region split and unorganized. Some day I may return the letters sent me over the years insisting that I favor toll roads and toll bridges as the salvation for Eastern Carolina.

"In January of 1959 the two bridges were as dead as the proverbial dodo bird. We entered the movement almost without hope but were determined to put forth our every effort. We quickly decided upon one thing and on that we were unanimous as we were on all other things -- there would be no toll roads or toll bridges anywhere in North Carolina if we could prevent it. We had lived under the burdensome influence of toll bridges, and we were not going to yield to people who had never weighed the question or realized what the effect would be. So, we quickly repealed all laws on the books that would authorize tolls anywhere in the State. In appearing before the State Highway Commission, of which that outstanding young man, J. Melville Broughton, Jr., was Chairman, we agreed there would be no delegations, and that there would be no personal lobbying of the members of the Commission by any of us. In our four appearances we based our arguments on facts, on geography and necessity. It was such an unusual course only one time did it get in the papers.

"We were not engaged on any political mission. We were crusading for a vast section of the State and to make it a part of the Commonwealth. A week after the General Assembly of 1959 adjourned the Commission acted and decided to build the two great toll free bridges. We shall never forget them. After the whole eastern section had been freed of tolls, after Governor Ehringhaus had said that only a free bridge would be built over Albemarle Sound; after Governor Umstead in announcing the construction of Croatan Sound Bridge had said, "no one will ever say that Bill Umstead built any toll bridge or toll road in North Carolina'; after these bridges authorized under the Hodges administration were announced as toll free, it has amazed us to read that two members of the present highway commission favored tolls on the Oregon Inlet Bridge. Such could only come through an utter lack of knowledge of the situation not only here but in the State. If such a thing would happen it would mean blowing up the Cape Hatteras Seashore where over a million people a year will visit after that bridge is completed. But I am not worried about that. It will never happen, for our great State never yet has gone back on its pledged word....

"As one who has lived with this coastal section for 45 years let me tell you as a fact that but for Fort Raleigh, the Lost Colony, the Wright Memorial and the Cape Hatteras National Seashore and the great National Park Service under the administration of Conrad L. Wirth, one of the Nation's foremost administrators, this bridge and the one across Oregon Inlet would only have been in the making for many, many years to come. Nowhere else in North Carolina should a people be more grateful to the Federal and State governments for all both have done for us. We should love our great State with a passionate devotion. We are all one great people -- the East -- the Piedmont -- and the West. We should become a part of its leadership and forward march. Every section has its problems but they should not breed sectionalism. We are still a rural state but there should be a happy balance between rural and what we know as urban. We should despise demagoguery and we should remember that unselfish public service in education, in agriculture, in industry and in civic upbuilding is after all the greatest satisfaction that can come to anyone."

I was privileged to work closely with Messrs. Warren and Bonner in connection with the dedication of these two bridges. I have often heard it said that Mr. Warren, having the inside track on the procurement of huge tracts of beach for the National Park Service, was in a position to have made for himself millions, but out of his dedication for the Outer Banks and its people, he chose not to pad his own pockets but to continue to serve the people he loved and who loved him.

In the 1930's when Mr. Warren was still in Congress, the Warren family would spend two weeks each summer in a rented cottage at Nags Head. Mrs. Warren traded with Adams Supply Co. in Washington and would order a two-week supply of groceries to be delivered at the cottage on July 4, and we'd make a real holiday of it. I worked for Bill Peele, manager of the store, and we would load the Dodge pickup truck with the groceries, and along with Dumay Toler and Joe Taylor, who clerked at the store, we'd take off at 4:00 A. M. driving up US 17 to Elizabeth City, over to Sligo and down through Currituck to Point Harbor, across the bridge to Kitty Hawk and on down to Nags Head. The Wright Memorial had just been erected and we'd always visit this magnificent edifice honoring the first flight on our way to the Warren cottage. The Warrens would have us stay for lunch and a swim in the ocean before our return trip. If time would permit we'd fish off one of the fishing piers in the vicinity. As far as I am concerned Lindsay Warren will go down in history as one of the greatest sons of Beaufort County to have ever lived, following in the footsteps of his father, Charles F. Warren, and grandfather, Edward Kidder Warren who gave of themselves and talents for the people of this area and this great State. Their portraits hang in a prominent place in the Superior Courtroom of Beaufort County Courthouse, and nearby is that of Herbert C. Bonner. I hearken back to those words of Mr. Warren at the bridge dedication when he said that public service is, after all, the greatest satisfaction that can come to any person.

Aerial view of Wright Memorial, Kill Devil Hills, N. C., August, 1940.
(Photo Courtesy of N. C. Division of Archives and History)

AFTERWORD

The phone rang. It was Cousin Mary (Styron) Akers calling from White River Junction, Vt.

"My precious Rick died," she sobbed, "and I want you to come to Hatteras next week and have a eulogy at memorial services in the Hatteras Methodist Church."

Rick and his brother Kevin had grown up at Hatteras when their father, Frederick McCarthy, operated a neighborhood grocery and their mother, Mary, taught school. After schooling at The University of Maryland, Rick moved back to Hatteras where he was close to the water and the people he loved. Later he moved back to Vermont to be near his family. Then a tragic end to a young life.

As we sat in the living room talking about old times and of the many family members who had gone on, childhood memories and experiences once again surfaced. Good times and sad times were remembered. Then, it was time to go to the church.

Rick's ashes were interred alongside the remains of his maternal grandparents, Charlie and Janie Styron, in the cemetery behind the Signal Office in the middle of Hatteras Village.

On one of the tombstones is inscribed, "Gone, But Not Forgotten."

Oh, Hatteras, you will live forever in my memories!

Index

ABC Stores 12
Adams, Monnie, Jr. 17
Adams Supply Co. 11,14,19,165
Adler, Richard 28
Akers, Mary Styron 167
Albatross, Boat 94
Albemarle Sound 52, 157,160,163
Alligator River 156,162
Alligator River Bridge 158,160
Alspaugh, Frank 21
Angell Cemetery 79
Angell, Inez 77
Angell, Lou 77
Angell, Nelson Paul 77
Angell, Tom 77,78,79,81
American Red Cross 115
Armed Services 26
Armstrong, Carl 35
Armstrong, Rufus 35,36
Arabian Horses 142
Asheville, N. C. 27
Assembly of God 144
Atlantic Ocean 39, 108
Atlantic View Hotel 71,98
Attorney General 20
Aunt Agnes 41
Aunt Mable 74, 109, 110, 142
Aurora, N. C. 8
Austin, Ander 41
Austin, Andrew 70
Austin, Ben 71
Austin, Horton 39
Austin, Kit 41
Austin, Russell 119
Avon, 41, 138, 139, 148

Bailey, N. C. 15
Balfour, L. G. & Co. 23
Ballance, Ellsworth 72, 98, 148
Ballance, Isaiah 46, 139
Ballance, Loren 70
Ballance, Reuben 70

Ballance, William Allen 119
Baltimore, Md. 1, 4
Barber, Richard 130

Barbara (Hurricane) 114
Bates Lumber Co. 7
Bath Town 1, 127, 131, 132
Bay River 4
Beacon, The 72, 148
Beacon Island Harbor 127
Beaufort, N. C. 90, 93
Beaufort County 19, 159
Beaufort County Arts Council 53
Beaufort County Commissioners 8
Beaufort County Courthouse 8, 165
Beaufort County Health Department 107
BHM Library 8, 9
Beaufort County Register of Deeds Office 127
Belhaven, N. C. 98
Belhaven Pilot Newspaper 120
Bell Family 9
Ben's Creek 81
Berry, D. L. 115
Bessie Virginia, Boat 43
Bierman's Department Store 24
Blounts Bay 1, 39
Blount, John Gray 2
Blount, Thomas 2
Blount, William 2
"Bloody Bucket" 72
Blue Marlin Marina 94, 139
Bodie Island 158
Bodie Island Lighthouse 50, 161
Bonner, Herbert C. 156, 159, 160, 165
Bonner, Col. James 1
Bonner Street 7
Bonnie Belle, Boat 57, 61, 86
Book Ex 20, 21, 23, 26
Boston, New England 1, 127, 131
Bowen, Pop 117
Bowman, Freddie 25
Boyd, Robert, Esq. 129, 131
Braddy, Geneva 37, 138
Brant Island 52
Briley, Charlie 21
British Ambassador 154
Broadway 28
Brooks, D. R. 23
Broughton, Gov. 159
Broughton, J. Melville, Jr. 163

169

Broughton, Sen. J. Melville 30
Brown, Dr. E. M. 145
Bull Durham 148
Burrus, Calvin 58
Burrus, Dolph's Wharf 67
Burrus, Dolph 70
Burrus, Lovie 109
Burrus, Maurice 148
Burrus, Richard (Dick) 119
Burrus, Roscoe 71
Buxton, N. C. 46, 50, 124, 139, 148
Buxton Woods 126

Camp Charles 15
Campbell, Madame E. T. 13
Canal, The 88
Cape Fear River 52
Cape Hatteras 129
Cape Hatteras Lighthouse 50, 124, 158
Cape Henry 129
Cape Hatteras National Seashore 151, 155, 156, 158, 164
Cape Hatteras School 101
Cape Hatteras Seashore 164
Cape Hatteras Weather Bureau 124
Carmichael, W. D. 25
Carolina Marching Band 25
Carolina Concert Band 25
Carolina Co-Op House 27
Carolina Theater 26
Carolina Inn 25
Carroll A. Deering, Ship 119, 120
Carroll, Dean Dudley DeWitt 35
Caribbean 108
Carteret County 51
Catholic School 13
Cedar Keys, Florida 5
Chamber of Commerce 7
Chapel Hill, N. C. 19, 35, 114
"Charlie Mason Pogie Boat", Song 90, 91
Cherry, William Downs 127, 128, 129
Chesapeake Bay 8, 53
Chincoteague, VA 142
Chitendon, Isaac 127
Chocowinity, N. C. 17
Chowan River Bridge 156
Cicero 13

City Market 44
City Shoe Hospital 17
Civil War 53
Clark, Ed 27
Coast Guard 49, 50, 154, 155
Coast Guard Picket Boat 90
Coastland Times 138, 162
Coastal N. C. 49
Coca Cola Bottling Plant 44
Cochrane, Bill 32
Cohoon, Charles 162
Columbia, N. C. 116, 162
Commissioner of Revenue 52
Comptroller General 156
Connie (Hurricane) 114
Congress 155
Cordouan, France 50
Core Sound 82
Core Sounders 91
Corolla 99
County of Beaufort 127
County Emergency Preparedness 117
Coquina Beach 158
Cox, Ship 119
Cox, George L. 116
Cratt, Miss Eva 107
Croatan Lighthouse 52
Croatan Sound 156
Croatan Sound Bridge 157, 160, 163
Crystal Ice Co. 44
Currituck 165
Currituck County
Currituck Twp (Hyde County) 115

Daily Advance 137
Daily Tar Heel 28
Dare Coast 152, 160
Dare County 153, 154
Dare County Board of Commissioners 125
Dare County Times 137, 138
Davenport, Julian 7
Day, Ryon 43
Defense Department 126
Delamar, Ned 162
Delco Plants 50
Denny, George V. Jr. 31, 32
Diamond Shoals 36, 119, 120, 149
Diamond Shoals Lightship 65, 149

Dianne (Hurricane) 114
Dolphin, Ship 127, 128, 129
Doppler Radar System
Dorsey, Tommy 24
Drane, Dr. 30
Drewer, H. C., Boat 41
Driscoll, Dave 43, 81
Dryden, Boat 43
Duke-Carolina 17
Duke Hospital 16, 17
Durham Coca Cola Bottling Co. 24
Durham's Creek 43, 44

Eason, Herman 17
East Coast 4, 108
East Lake 42, 72
Eaton, Tom 45
Edenton 130
Edenton Episcopal Church 30
Ehringhaus, Gov. 157, 163
Electric Membership Coop 46
Elizabeth City, N. C. 39, 58, 85, 86, 155, 165
Elizabeth City High School Band 157
Elizabeth City Independence 158
Endeavor, Sloop
Engelhard 45, 86, 98, 115, 138
Engelhard Bus Co. 116
Engelhard Creek 109, 114
Episcopalian 30
Episcopal Church of the Cross 30
Ernst, Roger C. 158
Ethel, Boat
Etheridge, R. Bruce 155, 162
Everett, Frank 162
Eureka Lumber Co. 7
Eureka, Tugboat 7
European Theater of Action 28

Fairfield, N. C. 115
Fairfield School 116
Faircloth, Sen. Lauch 125
Fall Germans 24
Farrow, Clyde 51
Farrow, Ezekial 130
Farrow, Jacob 130
Federal Aviation Agency 126

Federal Point (Near New Inlet) 52
First Baptist Church 16
First Congressional District 159, 160
First National Bank 57
First Order Lens 50
First United Methodist Church 23
Fletcher, Maynard O. 145
Florence Kerosene Stove 96
Florida 108
Flossie Muir, Boat 41, 43, 47, 54, 70
Foster, Bill 94
Foster, Charlie 94
Foster, Ernul 94
Foster, Gaston 94
Foster, Hallis 94
Foster, Lewis 21
Foster, Sue 94
Fort Raleigh 164
Fourth Order Lens 50
Fowle's Dock 2, 44, 57
Fowle, S. R. & Co. 2
Free Bridges 162, 163
Freeman, Grover 13
Freeman, Vernon 13
Fresnel, Augustin 49
Fresnel Lens 49, 50
Frisco, N. C. 148
Frying Pan Shoals 150
Ft. Raleigh 154
Futrell, Ashley 139
Galaway, Philip 127, 128, 129
Garrish, Powers "Red" 43
Garrish, Jesse 43
Gaskill, Walter 119
Gaskins, Ben 82
Gaskins, Ebby 82
Gaskins, Eldon 74, 82
Gaskins, Keith 82
Gaskins, Rosa 82
Gaskins, Walton 83
Georgia, State of 9
General Seafoods 7
Germantown Bay 4
Gimghoul Rd. 21, 26
Gladden St. 44
Goose Creek 81
Gooseville Gun Club 43, 65, 78, 81, 88
Gordon, Tugboat

Governor's Mansion 157
Graham, Dr. Frank 29, 30, 31
Graham, Mrs. Marian 29
Grandma Millie 62
Grandpop Irv 81, 89, 109, 133
Grandpap's Island 47
Gray, Damon 71, 133
Gray, Harold 71
Great Depression 19, 85
Great Lakes Naval Training Station 36
Green Island Gun Club 97
Green, Paul 155
Greenville, N. C. 1, 21
Guest, Raymond R. 159
Gulf Coast 4
Gulf Oil Dealer 69
Gulf of Mexico 5
Gull Shoal 52
Gulf Stream 108

Hadeco, Freight Boat 45, 138, 139
Hamilton, Alexander 52
Harbor Island 52
Harvey, Uncle 109
Hackler, Dr. R. H. 16
Harding, Edmund H. 5, 35
Harding, Rena "Peepie" 7
Hatch, Hurst 25
Hatteras 4, 15, 28, 39, 50, 85, 133, 138,
    139, 148, 151
Hatteras Development Co. 45, 139
Hatteras Inlet 1, 39, 86, 89, 97, 120, 147
Hatteras Inlet Coast Guard Station 59, 81
Hatteras Island 161
Hatterasmen 57, 113
Hatteras Methodist Church 167
Hatteras Mosquitoes 107
Hatteras Pilot 105
Hatteras Shoals 105
Havanna 129
Hendersonville, N. C. 27
Herbert C. Bonner Bridge 151
Hertford, N. C. 144
Hertford County 106
Highway 17 50, 44
Hoboken 44, 50

Hodges, Gov. Luther 158, 161
Hodgkins, Jonathan 129
Holston Conference 145
Holyoak, Samuel 131, 132
Horseshoe Shoal 52
Hospital Savings 27
House, R. B. 23, 32
House of Representatives 125
Howard, Sir Esme 154
Hoyt, James E. 2
Hurdle Mills, N. C. 29
Hurricane Barbara 117
Hurricane Connie 117
Hurricane Dianne 117
Hurricane Ione 117
Hurricane Hazel 114, 117
Hyde County 101
Hyde County Herald 115, 117

Ice Houses 67, 68
Inland Waterway 5
Insurance Commissioner 19
Ione (Hurricane) 114
Iowa, Boat 41
International Chimney Corp. of Buffalo, N.Y.
    124, 125

Jack's Creek 117
James, Harry 25
Japanese 26
Jarvis, J. H. 116
John Small School 11
Johnson, Dr. Cecil 24
Johnson, Earl 109
Johnson's Printing House 57
Jones, Rev. Charles 30
Jones, Rep. Walter, Jr. 125
June Germans 24

Kathleen, Freight Boat 39
Kemp, Hal 25
Kenan Stadium 24
Kenfield, Dr. John 55, 84, 100, 101
King George of Great Britain 127, 131
Kill Devil Hill 155
Kitty Hawk 44, 99, 153, 154, 160, 165

Kugler, F. C. 153, 154
Ku Klux Klan 74
Kyser, Kay 25

Lake Forest, Illinois 36
Lake Landing 116
Lange, Coach Bill 27
Lanier, Ed 19, 23
Laurel Point 52
Lenoir Dining Hall 26
Lexington, N. C. 21
Lighthouse Service 65
Linden, Buoy Tender 50
Linguistor 129
Little, Mrs. Clarence 17
Little, Sadie 17
Lombardo, Guy 25
London 127
Long, Johnny 25
Long Shoal 52
Lost Colony 155, 164
Louisiana Coast 4
Lyle Gun 92
Lynhaven Bay 129
Lyon, Albert, Sr. 78, 81

Mack, Connie 148
MacKenzie, R. P (Mack) 7
Maier, W. K. 5
Mallison, Freight Boat 41, 43
Maola Ice Cream Co. 44
Mallette, Mable 23
Mallette St. 27
Manns Harbor 115
Mann, Max 114
Manteo 44, 49, 74, 99, 139
Manteo Shipyard 60
Martha, Boat 99
Marines 27
Mary Fletcher, Freight Boat 39, 47, 54, 69, 70
Maryland 53
Mason, Connie 90
Mason, Jim 28
Massengill, S. E. & Co. 26
McCarthy, Frederick 71

McCarthy, Mary 71
McCarthy, Kevin 71
McCarthy, Rick 71
McKee, George 35
McLean, Gov. Angus W. 153
McMullan, Hon. Harry 20, 145
McMullan, Jim 20
McMullan, "Miss" Patty 20
Meekins, Edison 139
Meekins, John 70
Meekins, John, Wharf 67
Meekins, Milton 45, 139
Meekins, Nancy Jane 139, 143
Meekins, Victor 137, 138
Mellon Foundation 156
Mellon, Paul 159
Methodist Church 70, 116, 143
Methodist Episcopal Church 145
Methodist Episcopal Church (South) 145
Methodist Parsonage 101
Middletown, Hyde County 116
Midgette, Anderson 151
Midgette, Edison 51
Midgette, Harold 151
Midgette, Stockton 151
Miller, Ann 36
Miller, Glenn 24
Miss Ursula, Boat 149
Miss Yvonne, Boat 43, 65
Model A Ford 63, 106
Model T Ford 63
Moore, Adm. H. C. 159
Moore, James 13
Morehead City 90
Morgan, George 11
Morgan, John 31, 139, 140, 145
Morgan, Richard 47, 145
Morgan, Russ 25
Moss Planing Mill 4
Myers, John 2

Nags Head 31, 99, 154, 161, 165
National Hurricane Center 108
National Park Service 124, 125, 126, 164
National Register of Historic Sites 8
Navy Pre-Flight 24
Navy V-12 25, 27
NBC Line 7

173

N. C. Cafeteria   23
N. C. Ferry Dock   88
N. C. Highway 12   142
N. C. Lighthouses   52
N. C. Maritime Museum   90
N. C. Outer Banks   158
N. C. Pulp Co.   7
Neal, Lon   81
Neal, Sammy   41, 47, 54
New Berne   105
Nebraska, Hyde County   116
Nebuchadnezzar   83
Neuse River, Mouth of   4, 52
New Haven, Ct.   27
Newport, N. C.   126
Newsome, Willie   72
New York   1
Noe, Rev. A. C. D.   2
Norfolk, VA   1, 4, 7, 86, 126
Norfolk-Southern Trestle 39, 47
Nordan, Francis   27
Northeasters   114
Northern Methodist Church   143
North River, Mouth of   52
North Shores   7
Nunnelee, Jimmy   15
NW Point of Royal Shoal   52

Oak Island   52
Ocracoke 4, 43, 90, 100, 105, 121, 142, 148, 153
Ocracoke Barr   128
Ocracoke Ferry Service   43
Ocracoke Inlet   1, 127
Ocracoke Island 46, 81, 97, 142, 151
Ocracockers   57
Ocracoke Lighhouse   50
Oden, Dan   70
Oden, Deck   144
Oden, Herbert 41, 54
Oden, Julia   69
Oden, Melvin   13
Oden, Rance   69
Oden, Rance, Wharf   67
Old East   27
Old West   27
"Old Sea Captain and the Dummer", The   138
"Ole Bill", goat   63

Olivers Reef   50, 52, 146
Olivers Reef Lighthouse   77
O'Neal, Ansley   92
O'Neal, Capt. Ike   43
O'Neal, Capt. Johnny   54
O'Neal, Dick   162
O'Neal, Isaac "Little Ike"   43
O'Neal, Johnny   41
O'Neal, Vann Henry   43
O'Neal, Walter   43

Oregon Inlet 39, 44, 50, 138, 151, 156, 162, 164
Oregon Inlet Bridge   158, 160, 163
Oregon Inlet Ferry   158
Order of the Grail   24
Original Washington, N. C. 20
Outer Banks   28, 39, 81, 89, 117, 155
Outer Bankers   114, 133

Pacific Theater   49
Pamlico Chemical Dock 44
Pamlico Ice & Electric Co.   115
Pamlico Point 48
Pamlico Point Lighthouse 48 52, 54
Pamlico River 39, 48, 107, 117
Pamlico Sound 39, 48, 52, 53, 81, 105, 117, 124
Pamlico Shipyards   4, 5
Pasquotank Port City 58
Pasquotank River   39
Patterson Indoor Pool   24
Pattie Martin, Boat   120, 121
PCS Phosphate   8
Pearl Harbor   26
Peele, Bill   12, 165
Peele, Etta   99
Peele, Frazier 45, 151
Peele, Litchfield   97
Peele, Maxine   99
Peele, Rudolph 97, 99
Peele, Wesley   99
Peel, Sen. Elbert, Jr.   162
Perquimmans County   51
Person County   29
Phelps, Dr. J. M.   162
Philadelphia   1, 4

174

Philadelphia Athletics 148
Phillips Fertilizer Co. 4
Phipps Family 159
Phipps, Henry 158
"Pilot of Hatteras" 103
Pleasanton, Stephen 53
Plymouth, N. C. 11

Point Harbor 44, 160, 165
Port Terminal 1
Portugese Man-O-War 83
Potts, Joseph 2
Preacher Winslow 144
Pre-Flight 25
Presbyterian 30
Preston, Boat 43
Pully, Pete 24, 25
Putnam, George R. 53

Raleigh 27, 29
Red Cross 118
Register of Deeds 20, 36, 139
Relief, Boat 43
Respess Street 44
Rickards, Joe 117
"Ridge", The 106
Riensett, John 127
Ritchie, Ray 20, 23
River Road 13
Riverview, Tugboat 7
Roanoke Island 154, 155
Roanoke Marshes 52
Roanoke Marshes Lighthouse 49, 51
Roanoke Railroad & Lumber Co. 4
Roanoke River, Mouth of 52
Roanoke Sound 49
Robinson, Hubert 29
Robinson, Lee 70, 88
Rodanthe 138
Rodman, Cam 27
Roebuck, Leon 11
Roper, John L. Lumber Co. 7
Rose Bay 4
Roosevelt, President Franklin D. 25, 155
Royster Fertilizer Co. 4
Ruble, E. F. 22, 145
Rumley, Gilbert 20
Rumley, Henry 64

Rumley Motor Supplies 64
Rural Electrification Administration 46
Ruth, Boat 41

Saipan 27
Salvation Army 117
Sanders, Archie 4, 5
Sanders, Mrs. Archie 7
Sanders, Mrs. Kate 31
Sanford, Gov. Terry 161
Sarah, Sloop 129
Satterfield, Johnny 25
Saunders, W. O. 138, 159
Savage, Norman 23
Scarborough, Agnes 62
Scarborough, Edward 41
Scarborough, George 130
School of Commerce 35
Scott, Gov. Kerr 30, 156
Screw Pile Lighthouses 49
Scuttlebutt, The 25
Seaboard Coastline Railroad 29
Sea Chest, The 101
Sea Fever iv
Sears & Roebuck 143, 144
Seashore Park 160
Second Senatorial District 158
Secretary of Treasury 53
Sermons, Wayland 162
Shelton, Liz 16
Shelton, Mrs. Warren 16
Shytle, Ed 27
Shytle, Katherine 27
Signal Office 112, 167
Slash, The 101
Sligo 44, 165
Smithfield, N. C. 27
Smith, Capt. Dennis M. 121
Smith, Harvey 92
Smith, Willis 30
South Building 23, 24
South Creek 43
Southern Albemarle Association 160
Southern Comfort Range 96
Soule Methodist Church 116
Southern Methodist Church 143
Spaniards 129

Spanish Privateer   129
Spencer, Tom   115
Spencer Womens Dorm   30
Sports Editor   36
Square Dances   32
State Ferry Docks   93
State Highway Commission   163
State Highway Department   138
State Magazine   77
State Rehabilitation Commission   19
State of North Carolina   159
State Senate   139, 153
Steelman, Harrison J.   121
Sterling's Fish Market   44
Sterling, J. E., Freight Boat   41
Stewart, Ed   10
Stewart Family   9
Stewart Parkway   10
Stewart, R. Lee, Sr.   10
Stewart, Thomas   10
Stick, David   120
Stick, Frank   159
Stowe, Berry   49
Stowe, Billy   39
Stowe, Charles   89, 90
Stowe, Dallas   141
Stowe, Elmo   89
Stowe, Fannie   82
Stowe, Fred   89
Stowe, Frederick   89
Stowe, Harvey Doxey   60, 61
Stowe, Henry B.   119
Stowe, Irv   4, 70
Stowe, Janette   4, 39, 63, 70, 99, 100, 140
Stowe, John Irvin   39
Stowe, Lewis   89
Stowe, Maynard   149
Stowe, Millard   70
Stowe, Myron (Clam)   149
Stowe, Nelson   149
Stowe, Preston   4, 43, 64
Stowe, Randolph   41, 47
Stowe, Roland   63, 66
Stowe, Rube   81, 141, 145
Stowe, Walter   141, 145, 146
Stowe, William   65
St. Augustine   129
St. Thomas Episcopal Church   2
Studebaker Engine   57

Styron, Charlie   167
Styron, Edgar   94
Styron, George L.   119
Styron, Jane   119
Styron, Janie   167
Styron, Litchfield   119
Summerlin, Sam   25
Superior Courtroom   165
SW Point of Royal Shoal   52
Swan Quarter   115, 116

Tarboro   1, 2
Tar River   1
Tayloe, Dr. David T.   37
Tayloe Drug Store   19
Tayloe Hospital   15, 16, 17
Tayloe, Dr. Josh   17
Tayloe Hospital School of Nursing   37
Taylor, Joe   165
Terrell, Robert L.   120
Texasgulf   8
Texas Towers   150
"The Three Stooges"   82
Thrall, Dr. Frank   21
Thrall, Mrs. Frank   21
Tillett, Toby   44
Tin Can   24
Toler, Dumay   165
Toll Bridges   162, 163
Tolson, George   121
Tolson, Sid   43
Tory, David   129, 130
"Town Hall Meeting of the Air"   31
Tunstall, Joe   19
Two Friends, Brigantine   131
Tyrrell County   72

Umstead, Gov. William B.   157, 163
Umstead Memorial Bridge   158
Uncle Berry   82, 83
Uncle Harvey   43, 82, 86, 106, 113, 138, 143

University Club   24
University of Maryland   167
University Presbyterian Church   30
UNC - Chapel Hill   19, 109
UNC School of Pharmacy   19

176

UN Security Council 30
Urban Renewal 9
U. S. Bureau of Lighthouses 53
U. S. Coast Guard 53, 124
U. S. Corps of Engineers 1
U. S. Lighthouse Service 53
U. S. Mail Truck 116

Vandemere Trestle 39
VE Day 35
VEP Co. 46
VJ Day 35
Verbena, Buoy Tender 50
Vince, Thomas 77
Virgil 13
Virginia Beach 156
Virginia Capes 108
Virginia Dare 154
Virginian Pilot 137

Wade's Point Lighthouse 52
Wadley, Joseph 131, 132
Wahab, Stanley 93
Wakely, Samuel 129
Wall, Joshua 130
Wallack, Dick 27
War Between the States 144
War Labor Board 29
Warner, Bill's Railways 7
Warren, Lindsay C. 152, 153, 154, 155, 156, 157, 158
Warren, Charles F. 165
Warren Family 165
Warren, Edward Kidder 165
Warren, Lindsay C. Bridge 162
Washington 1, 7, 11
Washington, Town Of 4, 86, 107, 116
Washington Buoy Yard 50, 51, 90
Washington Collegiate Institute (WCI) 22, 145
Washington Daily News 11, 19, 36, 115, 139, 161
Washington, D. C. 29
Washington High School 19, 145
"Washington on the Air" 35
Washington Park 145
Washington Tobacco Market 7, 35

Waters, Bill 11
Watson's Chapel Methodist Church 116
Way, George 127, 128, 129
WCTU (Womans Christian Temperance Union) 12
Weather Bureau 112
Weather Service 126
Welch Ward, (Duke Hospital) 17
West Indies 1, 2
Weyerhaeuser Co. 7
Whalebone Junction 44
Whealton, Lee 15
Whealton, Melvin 15
Wheeler, Col. John Hill 106
Whichard, Warren (Big Time) 15
White Cane Gift Shop 63, 66
White Phantoms (UNC Basketball Team) 27
Whitfield, Cy 29
White River Jct. Vt. 167
Williamston, N. C. 11
Williams, Dave 43
Williams, Phil 43
Williams, Travis 93
Willis, Irish 70
Willis, Irish Wharf 67
Willis, John 145
Willis, Mike 47
Willis, Pete 69
Willis, Phil 47
Willis, S. P. & Sons
Willis, S. P. Dock 47
Willis, S. P. Family 47
Willis, S. P. Fish House 69
Willis, Tom Grace 51
Wilmington, N. C. 126
Winslow, Preacher 144
Winston-Salem, N. C. 21
Wirth, Conrad L. 156, 158, 164
Wittick, Roy J. 7
Womens College 31
Wood, George Henry 51
Wood, Josh Kingsley 51
Woolen Gym 24
Woolworth's Department Store 147
World War II 24, 49, 74, 99
Worley, Fish 32
Wright Brothers 154
Wright Memorial 155, 164, 165

Wright Memorial Bridge 156
WHED Radio Station 32, 36
WRRF Radio Station 32, 35

"Y" Court 24
Young, Payton 92

ZBT Fraternity 28